The Gospel According to PEANUTS.

by Robert L. Short

Foreword by Nathan A. Scott, Jr.

JOHN KNOX PRESS
Atlanta, Georgia

To My Parents—
who, I am sure, in struggling
to cultivate their own
little patch of peanuts,
have acquired real appreciation
for the full meaning of
"Good grief!"

30
Scripture quotations are from the Revised Standard Version, copyright 1946 and 1952 by the Division of Christian Education of the National Council of the Churches of Christ in the U.S.A.

Cartoons copyright 1955, 1956, by United Feature Syndicate, Inc., copyright © 1957, 1958, 1959, 1960, 1961, 1962, 1963, 1964 by United Feature Syndicate, Inc. Used by permission.

ISBN: 8042-1968-0
Library of Congress Catalog Card Number: 65-11632
© M. E Bratcher 1965
Printed in the United States of America

Contents

Acknowledgments

There are several pen-pals and many neighborhood friends whose help and encouragement I would like to acknowledge. My most excellent teachers, Doctors Nathan A. Scott, Jr., and Preston Roberts, Jr., of the Department of Theology and Literature in the Divinity School of The University of Chicago, have evidently understood the difficulties of their task and yet have not been disheartened by them. They have met the enemy, and he is me. Their patience with me as a student (and graciousness to me as a friend) are greatly appreciated. For many years now, A. R. Larreta has played a steadfast-in-encouragement Charlie Brown to my trembling and fearful Linus. The ideas and suggestions of friends James M. Brown, Norman A. Smith, G. W. Linden, Roger Ortmayer, Joseph W. Matthews, and B. J. Stiles have always been especially creative and stimulating for me. A special word of thanks is due to the many audiences who have seen the nucleus of this book presented in the form of a color-slide program. Their comments, questions, laughter, and frank discussions with me about *Peanuts,* and about the Christian message, have been helpful to me in countless ways. I am also greatly indebted to Mr. Schulz, the creator of *Peanuts,* and to the United Feature Syndicate for their kind permission to use *Peanuts* in this rather unusual form of "theological literary criticism"—illustrated.

R.L.S.

Foreword

A few years ago Reuel Denney entitled his fine book on American popular culture *The Astonished Muse,* and I suspect that that ancient tutelary must indeed be astonished by the purposes into the service of which Charles Schulz has so remarkably brought the art of the cartoon strip. This is, of course, a medium for which in the last decade or so we have often found it difficult to summon up the old affections of our childhood. For the kind of cheap catharsis that of late it has so frequently offered to an "affluent society" and its equally frequent dedication to the ugly iconography of rape and flagellation and murder have tended to provide ample confirmation of Frederic Wertham's severe conclusion, that the chief effect today of the comic book and the cartoon strip is a depraving "seduction of the innocent."

Yet it may well be that the kind of melodramatic horror with which we contemplate this material is sometimes too automatic, too reflexive, and that, as a result, our firm intention to be either patronizingly permissive or stringently hostile and censorious toward the very medium itself tends to blind us to the occasional triumphs that it achieves, of *esprit* and inventiveness and gaiety and fun. *Mad,* in its wildest moments, and *Superman* may, to be sure, strike us as unfortunate perversions of the kind of art that was finding expression a generation ago in *Little Orphan Annie* and *Dick Tracy* and *Gasoline Alley.* But, at the time when my own children had a far greater appetite for cartoon strips and comic books than they now have, though the "enlightened" side of my mind told me that I should prefer them to be reading the antiseptic little fables of Lois Lenski, I could at least be somewhat comforted by the thought that Walt Kelly was still doing *Pogo* for them, that Al Capp's *Li'l Abner* wasn't always objectionable, and that they needn't therefore be wholly reliant on "humor in a jugular vein."

And, as Robert Short is now reminding us, the art of the cartoon strip must not have been wholly corrupted if it can still afford a working medium for so scrupulous and lively an imagination as that of Charles Schulz. For, in and through the fabulous little world of Charlie Brown and Lucy and Linus and Snoopy and Shermy and Violet, Mr. Schulz has been turning a remarkably penetrating searchlight on the anxieties and evasions and duplicities that make up our common lot; and, as Mr. Short fully demonstrates in this attractive little book, the analysis of human existence that Mr. Schulz is giving us is essentially theological and, in its basic inspiration, deeply Christian. Indeed, it is by way of "the gospel according to *Peanuts*" that Mr. Short is himself enabled to reweave an interpretation of the Christian faith whose urbane simplicity will doubtless for many recall the apologetic style of C. S. Lewis: it is, in every way, a most engaging piece of writing, in its constructive theological aspect as well as in its interpretation of a significant body of popular art. And I expect that this book will quickly make a good place for itself in the affections of a large body of readers, both young and old.

Nathan A. Scott, Jr.
Professor of Theology and Literature
The Divinity School
The University of Chicago

Nay, but by men of strange lips and with an alien tongue the
LORD will speak to this people.

—*Isaiah 28:11*

But who is with him?
None but the fool, who labours to out-jest
His heart-struck injuries.

—*King Lear, III, i*

... if you do not say anything in a cartoon, you might as well not
draw it at all. Humor which does not say anything is worthless
humor. So I contend that a cartoonist must be given a chance to
do his own preaching.

—*Charles M. Schulz,*
creator of *Peanuts[1]*

I. The Church and the Arts

"How shall we sing the LORD's song in a foreign land?" (Ps.
137:4) is a question the Church, always finding itself *in* but not *of*
the world, urgently needs to reconsider today. For it not only needs
to reconsider how it can best make meaningful contact with the
particular men of our particular time, with all of their own idiosyn-
crasies; but the Church also needs to re-examine its strategy of communication to men of *all* times—since the objection *all* men have to
the Church's message is fundamentally the same: it is that universal
hardness of heart lying far more deeply and steadfastly within them
than any objection men can usually hold consciously. Paradoxically,
however, it is often the very *urgency* the Church has for its message
that brings the Church's proclamation running up against so many
brick walls. It is often the very bluntness and directness of the *approach* of the Church that in turn blunts or shatters the very delicate
opportunities it has for its message being heard; or blunts and shatters its own "two-edged sword," the gospel. And as Paul Tillich has
put it, "We all know the pain we suffer when we meet people who
reject the Gospel ... since the Gospel was never properly com-
municated to them."[2] The Church's characteristic approach (and the
rebuffs that characteristically result) are thus strongly analogous to
the following attempt at communication by Charlie Brown:

"Change your mind!" Charlie Brown pleads over and over in a similar scene with similar results: "It's almost impossible to get people to change their minds these days!"

More than any other modern thinker, Søren Kierkegaard saw and wrestled with the problems of communicating the Christian message. He finally advocated a strategy of "indirect communication" in which "one does not begin thus: I am a Christian; you are not a Christian. Nor does one begin thus: It is Christianity I am proclaiming; and you are living in purely aesthetic categories. No, one begins thus: Let us talk about aesthetics. The deception consists in the fact that one talks thus merely to get to the religious theme."[3] But why "deception"? Because:

> If one is to lift up the whole age one must truly know it. That is why those ministers of Christianity who begin at once with orthodoxy have so little effect and only on few. . . . One must begin

with paganism. . . . If one begins immediately with Christianity then they say: that is nothing for us—and they are immediately on their guard.[4]

On their guard, indeed! Just watch this little encounter between Linus and his sister, Lucy:

Of course someone might have scruples about Kierkegaard's notions of "deceiving" a person into the truth, or "beginning with paganism"—equally blasphemous! But a person with such objections should have his or her attention called to the "deceptions" St. Paul was willing to use in order that *he* "might win the more":

> To the Jews I became as a Jew, in order to win Jews; to those under the law I became as one under the law—though not being myself under the law—that I might win those under the law. To those outside the law I became as one outside the law. . . . To the

weak I became weak, that I might win the weak. I have become all things to all men, that I might by all means save some (1 Cor. 9:20-22).

Paul, like Kierkegaard, realized that in order to "save" men, one must begin at where they are—in "paganism." Man's *original* position in this world is always—unfortunately—in sin, otherwise man would certainly have no serious need for any kind of serious "salvation." Thus if a Christian is to "lift up" such a brother, he must be willing to stoop down; if he is to walk a second mile with his brother, he must be willing to go with him down some strange paths—just as God himself was willing to lower himself to becoming a man in order to "lift up" men. In the words of Irenaeus, God "did through his transcendent love become what we are, that he might bring us to be what he is himself."

Generally speaking, there are two barriers to modern man's understanding the Christian message—barriers that must be taken seriously by the Church in any strategy it conceives for the proclamation of its message. The *first* can be called the "intellectual" barrier because it consists of the fact that no clear-cut decision for or against the gospel has been made *possible* for the hearer. He is not even sure in his mind what the alternatives are. For the Church's "Words strain,/ Crack and sometimes break, under the burden,/ Under the tension, slip, slide, perish,/ Decay with imprecision, will not stay in place,/ Will not stay still."[5] But the Church is not only guilty of committing its gospel to a decayed and imprecise vocabulary; more importantly, it is also guilty of the sin of omission: often a very crucial part of its message is completely ignored or forgotten. For instance, "Be of good cheer!" is a phrase that probably leaves most of us cold nowadays. But this phrase was a byword in New Testament times, because it was invariably accompanied with some specific *reason for* being of good cheer, such as "Your sins are forgiven" (Matt. 9:2) or "I have overcome the world" (John 16:33). But how can "Be of good cheer!" have any comfort or meaning for us today when not only are we not sure what "Your sins are forgiven!" means, but often we are not even told that this is the case—"As though everything were not said in that phrase!"[6]

The *second* obstacle to man's understanding the Christian message is much deeper and more fundamental, for it concerns a difficulty with his heart rather than with his head. All men are created equal in at least one sense: "the imagination of man's heart is evil from his youth" (Gen. 8:21). We are all "constitutionally unable to love or under*stand* any son of God who throws tables around,"[7] as J. D. Salinger has put it. Or as expressed in Isaiah, "from birth you were called a rebel" (Isa. 48:8). The New Testament was certainly in agreement with this point of view (as we shall further see in the next chapter), and of course was well aware of the terrific obstacle its message faced at this wall of "constitutional" sin. Thus we find Christ quoting Isaiah by saying:

> You shall indeed hear but never understand, and you shall indeed see but never perceive. For this people's heart has grown dull, and their ears are heavy of hearing, and their eyes they have closed, lest they should perceive with their eyes, and hear with

their ears, and understand with their heart and turn for me to heal them (Matt. 13:14-15; Isa. 6:9-10).

Man then is trapped in his own blindness, in the circle of his own humanity. Apart from God's mercy, men cannot even "turn for [God] to heal them." This is why when a man *does* turn to God, this revolution, or reversal, always has the aspect of a *miracle*,[8] it is a revolution which occurs in *spite* of man's own best efforts rather than *because* of them.

And hence the great significance for all men of Christ's healing the man "born blind" (John 9). There is a sense in which *all* men are born blind, and it is *only* by God's mercy through Jesus Christ that this original or "birth" sin is overcome. For "never since the world began has it been heard that any one opened the eyes of a man born blind" (John 9:32).

Thus the Church should always remember that regardless of how much it may at times seem to have sharpened its language, making the alternatives of its message crystal clear *intellectually,* God "has mercy upon whomever he wills, and he hardens the heart of whomever he wills" (Rom. 9:18).

Art has a way of getting around man's intellectual and emotional prejudices. This is because art always speaks *indirectly*—whether in being the vehicle for delivering a new *answer,* or in causing a new kind of *question* to be asked that must be asked before any new answer can make sense.

Far too often the Church finds itself in the trap of attempting to explain its position in a language that is itself not meaningful. When Linus asks his mother why he cannot "slug" Lucy, who has taken his book of stories, his mother answers, "That's just one of those things I can't explain." But Lucy has an explanation: "Listen dope!" she tells Linus, with her fist in his face, "If you slug me, I'll slug you right back!!" "Never mind, Mom," says Linus after silently watching Lucy turn and walk away with his book; "It's just been explained to me in language I can understand." The Church's missionaries to its "cultured despisers" need to be as well acquainted with the current languages of culture as the Church's missionaries to foreign lands are acquainted with the languages of the areas into which they are sent. Art is one of the most eloquent and influential voices of any culture. It not only expresses the hopes, fears, and needs of a culture, but it also provides its own unique vocabulary of signs and symbols in which these needs are expressed. If the Church does not correlate its age-old answer with the ways in which man's age-old question is being asked both emotionally and intellectually, it is like the man who once invented the cure for which there was no disease. Thus "to make an apt answer is a joy to a man, and a word in season, how good it is!" (Prov. 15:23).

Art, just because of its subtlety or indirectness, has a way of sneaking around "mental blocks" and getting to the heart of the matter where it is capable of deeply and literally "moving"—even the most immovable—men and women.

Art can also aid in penetrating man's emotional prejudices by showing him who he really is; by accurately reflecting his own pretentions, foibles, and anxieties; by setting up before him a mirror where he may see his own inmost part.

In this sense, the purpose of art, as Shakespeare said of "the purpose of playing,"

> both, at the first and now, was and is, to hold as 'twere, the mirror up to nature; to show Virture her own feature, scorn her own image, and the very age and body of the time his form and pressure.[9]

Thus Snoopy, just as art, "holding the mirror up to nature" in the following cartoon, playfully manages "to show . . . scorn her own image":

Hence art, as a reflector, can also judge us in our very act of judging it. In making our decision about what it is, we reveal and define who we are. Works of art, as Lichtenburg said, "are mirrors: when a monkey peers into them, no Apostle can be seen looking out."[10] Art, like Christ, casts us back upon ourselves for a searching decision: "Who do *you* say that I am?" they ask. For in both cases, the answer is never self-evident.

Again, the artist is capable of bringing us into these honest confrontations with ourselves by *indirections*. He is not above sugar-coating the most bitter pill, above being "wise as serpents and innocent as doves" (Matt. 10:16), above cleverly disguising the truth in order to get it through the enemy's defenses. This is why all real art, though at first it may seem to be a most welcome escape *from* reality, will inevitably lead one into a face to face encounter *with* reality—but always with reality in a different light from which it was first seen. Thus Hamlet could say, "The play's the thing/Wherein I'll catch the conscience of the king";[11] or Denis De Rougemont can define art "as a *calculated trap for meditation.*"[12] Therefore many people—from statesmen to thieves—are sometimes suspicious of art. They have learned to be "on guard" even against the indirect approach:

Art can also bring about some radical shifts in one's *intellectual* presuppositions. It does this by providing "conversation pieces" that attract one's attention while moving the basis of conversation onto entirely new grounds. For the conversation pieces of art are *loaded* (and thus they "always have a way of backfiring") with entirely new sets of symbols or ways of looking at things. Again, these symbols suggest new *questions* or old *answers* seen from fresh perspectives.

"Conversation," then, arises between the work of art itself and the *observer* of the work who feels the work has somehow "spoken" to him; or the conversation can take place—and this is more often the case—between such an observer and the observer who does *not* feel spoken to by the work. At this point the Church should become acutely interested. For great is the number of people in our time who could not care less for having any kind of serious, direct discussion about the "Christian message" as such. But many of these same people would be perfectly delighted to carry on a discussion with anyone about any form of art and on any basis.

Therefore if there is some truth *in* art (and it must follow, as the night the day, that the greater the art the more truth-full it will be) that the Christian observer can point to, he can then by this means speak a word to his brother who might not be willing to listen in any other way. The artist, then, is like a man who is "speaking in strange tongues," to use Paul's language. The ability to speak in tongues Paul saw as one of the great "gifts of the Spirit" within the Church. For to one was given one gift, "to another various kinds of tongues, to another the interpretation of tongues" (1 Cor. 12:10), and so on. But, as Paul also pointed out, no one will be able to understand these tongues "if there is no one to interpret" (1 Cor. 14:28). Thus, the Church, rather than always being annoyed by the arts, should encourage a vanguard of men and women to be *interpreters* of these tongues, or arts, which can act as truly provocative "conversation pieces" between the Church and the culture in which the Church finds itself. This is why Paul could say that "tongues are a sign not for believers but for unbelievers" (1 Cor. 14:22), but that still their interpretation must come from the Church! As an example of the type of "conversation piece" art can be, suppose we take this cartoon, featuring Linus and his ever-present blanket:

Now, suppose we consider the kind of "conversation" which can arise from such a cartoon when it is interpreted by a member of the Church—in this case the artist himself:

> Linus' affection for his blanket . . . is a symbol of the things we cling to. . . . What I am getting at, of course, is the adult's inadequacy here—the inability to give up habits which really should be given up. Not that I am completely against the idea that we have to cling to something! For once you accept Jesus, it does not mean that all of your problems are automatically solved, or that you will never be lonesome or unhappy again. How can you be happy all the time, if you are aware of the things that are going on around you? But some of our adult habits are ridiculous.[13]

At this point I ought to mention that the Church should not always expect the artist to do his own interpreting as Mr. Schulz was frank enough to do in the above quotation. That is not the artist's job—just as Paul separates the work of *interpreters* of tongues and those who *speak* in tongues. If the artist felt it more important for him to speak directly, then he probably would not be an artist. As Schulz has said of his approach to the Sunday Bible class he teaches, the approach of most artists "is to create a climate in which people will . . . ask even little questions."[14] Thus we can certainly understand the occasional impatience artists have with the lack of perceptive interpreters, or "critics," who should be doing their share of the work—helping to provide an answer to the often pregnant questions posed by the artist; but even more can we understand the artist's impatience with those who even "will not learn to look," as E. E. Cummings has put it. Once while pitching a baseball game, Charlie Brown wanted his catcher, Schroeder, to ask him a certain encouraging question, but finally had to ask Schroeder to ask him the question, explain the question to Schroeder, and *then* give Schroeder the answer. Observed Charlie Brown: "It's terrible when you have to do everything yourself!" *Theoretically* at least, Christians have been given "the secrets of the Kingdom of heaven," have "eyes to see," "ears to hear," and "understanding in everything." It is surely easy enough for most Christians to see that "the biblical interpreter must go beyond the letter of Scripture to the meaning. He must seek 'the Word behind the words,' "[15] as Bernhard W. Anderson has said. But the Christian should be nominated for the world's worst sluggard if he uses his special gift for seeing only when he looks into Scripture—and how often is that?

Indeed, for the Christian "the whole earth is full of [God's] glory" (Isa. 6:3)—or should be. Even the so-called "secular philosopher" can see that a special kind of "seeing" is at the heart of the Christian point of view. For example:

> What appears to the common, profane view as the immediately given reality of 'things' is transformed by the religious view into a world of 'signs.' The specifically religious point of view is indeed determined by this reversal. All physical and material things, every substance and every action, now become metaphoric . . . expression of a spiritual meaning.[16]

Whenever the Church becomes too dull or narrow in using the gift of its spiritual perception, it is guilty of the same charge Christ laid to the Pharisees and Sadducees: "You know how to interpret the appearance of the sky, but you cannot interpret the signs of the times" (Matt. 16:3). At this point the Church will be of little help to—and in the same boat with—all the Lucys of the world; and they are legion:

But in addition to the concepts of "unknown tongues" and "signs of the times," there is another even more important biblical basis for this type of indirect, or "artistic," communication of the Christian message. The parables of Christ were an essential method of communicating Christ's gospel because of the very nature of this message itself. Hence "indeed he said nothing to them without a parable" (Matt. 13:34; Mark 4:34). But the parables were not simply clever homiletic devices or illustrations used to clear up a difficult point or two. As a matter of fact, their purpose seemed to be much closer to *creating* difficulties. Over and over in the Gospels we find statements such as, "And they did not understand the saying which he spoke to them" (Luke 2:50). In a sense the parables were actually used to *hide* the truth first, rather than to make it immediately apparent:

> Then the disciples came and said to him, "Why do you speak to them in parables?" And he answered them, "To you it has been given to know the secrets of the kingdom of heaven, but to them it has not been given ... but from him who has not, even what he has will be taken away. This is why I speak to them in parables, because seeing they do not see, and hearing they do not hear, nor do they understand (Matt. 13:10-13).

In order for a man to understand with his heart the truth, which is by nature completely foreign to his heart, something *first* must "be taken away" from his heart—namely, that hardness which surrounds his heart and prevents his "seeing," "hearing," "understanding." "The unspiritual man does not ... understand [spiritual truths] because they are spiritually discerned" (1 Cor. 2:14). But the parables are designed to help make this impossible discernment possible; they do this by presenting the "unspiritual man" with "riddles" (Prov. 1:6), or "dark sayings" (Ps. 78:2), calculated to crack him before he can crack them. The parables "not only arrest attention; they arouse something deep within."[17] For there is no way of accepting and appreciating the radical truth of the gospel unless one first has radical need of it; there is no way of receiving the answer of pure joy until the question is first asked in fear and trembling; one must truly *seek* before one "will find/Where truth is hid, though it were hid indeed/Within the centre."[18] And thus Christ could say that the lamp of the gospel is not finally "brought in to be put under a bushel. ... For there is nothing hid, except to be made manifest; nor is anything secret, except to come to light" (Mark 4:21-22). "Faith directs itself towards the things that are invisible," said Luther. "Indeed, only when that which is believed on is hidden, can it provide an opportunity for faith."[19]

Art can be understood as being a parable (and vice versa), for the indirect methods of both are identical. There are of course many works of art that are not "getting at" the same thing as the Christian message. Likewise, there may be nothing particularly "Christian" in intent about a landscape composed of "lilies of the field" and "birds of the air." Yet Christ was able to speak eloquently about his "heavenly Father" on basis of just such a landscape (Matt. 6; Luke 12). "The language of faith uses the language of culture even when it must transmute the meaning of that language."[20] Further, the language of faith will always find the language of art particularly appropriate. Both have a deeper, more passionate vision of reality than is commonly given; and both are bent on communicating something of this vision to the *heart* of man through forms which will stop his attention. The Church will always need "fresh" parables—whatever their original "intent"—in which to pour the "new wine" of the New Testament. For "no one puts new wine into old wineskins; if he does, the wine will burst the skins, and the wine is lost, and so are the skins; but new wine is for fresh skins" (Mark 2:22). Or, to use another biblical metaphor, as "fishers of men" Christians should learn to use more effectively some of the newer and better types of "bait" available to them.

Historically, however, the Church has been impatient with the arts, just as many of Christ's detractors were impatient with his parables and indirectness: "How long will you keep us in suspense? If you are the Christ, tell us plainly" (John 10:24). The same impatience has often caused the Church's strategy to be simply one of "turning up the volume" whenever it has felt that its message was not being heard. In its zeal to get a hearing, the Church has usually been addicted to the "hardsell" approach, forgetting that the greater part of the approach of Christ (*"a greater artist than all other artists,"* as Van Gogh said of him[21]) to winning men was decidedly quiet and indirect: it was to remold—partly through a very *human* kind of love—the lives of his disciples into *works of art,* through which the gentleness and kindness of their own love also was calculated to bring men to a saving knowledge of the love of *God.* For human love is not only analogous to the benevolence of God's love; but human love also can *break a man's heart,* thus making it possible for the originally hard but empty shell of man's heart then to be receptive *in depth* to God's love. This is why the Bible often speaks in a sort of "love your enemies—it'll kill them" sense. For instance, Paul is quoting the Old Testament when he says, "if your enemy is hungry, feed him; if he is thirsty, give him drink; for by so doing you will heap burning coals upon his head" (Rom. 12:20; Prov. 25:21-22).

But of course, the Church has felt, human love—just as the parables —can be a much too roundabout or "artful" way of proclaiming the love of God. Therefore, on with the "plain truth" and *up with the volume!*

The Church also has been traditionally suspicious of the artist be-cause of the artist's equally traditional honesty. Since the days when Christianity was itself an underground movement within a hostile Roman Empire, and hence could afford no complacency, many Christians have preferred to remain incognito subversives (and often as artists of one kind or another) in order to move deeply into the territory of the unbeliever, while all the time sniping away at a successful worldly and self-satisfied Church. But the Church has very cleverly protected itself against the charges of the artist by saying, "Look who's talking! This neurotic, unwashed beatnik!" or whatever the fashionable terms of abuse might be. (A generation ago, artists were merely a "bunch of uncouth Bohemians!") Such *ad hominem* arguments are probably the crab grass in the lawn of any artist's life:

Therefore if the artist is going to become more popular with the
Church, he may have to become less honest—or at least become more
diplomatic. For instance, in one *Peanuts* strip Lucy asks Charlie
Brown, "Do you think I'm a crabby person?" Charlie Brown, after
some consideration, replies frankly, "Yes, I think you're a very
crabby person." *"Well, who cares what you think?!"* she shouts at
him. The Church should never lay that flattering unction to its
soul that not its trespass but the artist's madness speaks. (For though
this *be* madness, yet there is method in it.) If today's Church really
is the world's largest non-prophet organization, it should welcome
these prophetic souls in the true spirit of the New Testament: "Do
not neglect to show hospitality to strangers, for thereby some have
entertained angels unawares" (Heb. 13:2). The Church has been
willing to use the arts in the past: but generally speaking that is *all*

it has done—it has *used* them, whether as decoration or as amusement or as simple and usually sentimental religious illustration or propaganda. Of all the things created by man, art is most like a man, it can contain more of a man's life: it is a synthesis of an extremely complex body or form together with incredibly deep passion. Therefore, like a man, art should not be used or seen as an *it,* but should be respected and heard as a *Thou.* And like a man, art—real art—will always have something to *say.* Therefore, in spite of our many natural attempts to avoid listening, all art should be listened to carefully.

Peanuts, the famous cartoon strip, often assumes the form of a modern-day, Christian parable. To illustrate how closely the parables of *Peanuts* can parallel the parables of the New Testament—in lessons suggested, in ways of suggesting these lessons, and in indirect method—the following cartoon is coupled with Christ's parable of "The house on the rock and the house on the sand" (Matt. 7:24-27):

"Every one then who hears these words of mine and does them will be like a wise man who built his house upon the rock; and the rain fell, and the floods came, and the winds blew and beat upon that house, but it did not fall, because it had been founded on the rock.

And every one who hears these words of mine and does not do them will be like a foolish man who built his house upon the sand; and the rain fell, and the floods came, and the winds blew and beat against that house,

and it fell; and great was the fall of it."

And so there *are* lessons to be found in *Peanuts;* but just as in the parables of Christ, we are not always sure what these lessons are. Or, as Lucy would put it, also in *Peanuts* we have trouble "reading between the lines." Mr. Schulz has said,

> ... naturally I must exercise care in the way I go about express-ing things. I have a message that I want to present, but I would rather bend a little to put over a point than to have the whole strip dropped because it is too obvious. As a result ... all kinds of people in religious work have written to thank me for preaching in my own way through the strips. That is one of the things that keep me going.[22]

We know, from materials written by and about Mr. Schulz,[23] that he is an extremely active "lay-preacher" of the Church of God (headquartered in Anderson, Indiana). He has confessed, as we have seen, to presenting something of a religious message in *Peanuts;* but evidently he has not gone much further in specifying exactly what this message is. Again, why should he? As I have attempted to make clear, the job of the interpreter (whether minister, priest, pro-fessional critic, or perceptive layman) and the job of the artist should usually be kept apart. "How can you give a personal evaluation of a work of art?" was Schulz's guarded reply when one reporter at-tempted to force him into becoming his own critic.[24] Both the Church and the artist must constantly beware of cheapening what they have to say by making it *too* accessible. "Remove from the Christian Religion, as Christendom has done, its ability to shock, and Christianity, by becoming a direct communication, is altogether destroyed. It then becomes a tiny superficial thing, capable neither of inflicting deep wounds nor of healing them . . ."[25]

That is to say, lessons "to be found," if they are to be seriously *appreciated* when found, will always first require a corresponding amount of serious *seeking.* And so then, like Charlie Brown, the job of Charles Schulz probably should not be the *interpretation* of "prophetic literature" as much as it is the *creation* of it:

Our purpose in the remaining chapters of this little book, will simply be to act as an interpreter of the delightful "unknown tongues" or "parables" or "prophetic literature" of *Peanuts.* In pointing to some of the themes and symbols that seem to run throughout *Peanuts,* we will simply be trying to say what *Peanuts* has said to us

—as a Christian interpreter. All art criticism or interpretation will
inevitably begin from such a personal point of view. "There is no
'impartial criticism' in this sense," writes S. L. Bethell; "... there is
no critical neutrality; there are only Christian critics and Marxist
critics and Moslem critics—and critics who think themselves dis-
interested but who are really swayed unconsciously by the beliefs
they have necessarily acquired by being members of a particular
society in a particular place and time."[26] Moreover, the meaning of
art, like the heart of a man, is never open to objective analysis—even
via the electronic computer. Scientific and historical analysis of art
and literature, such as the so-called "higher criticism" of biblical
scholarship, can be quite useful of course when applied to *objects*.
But to use this method on a human heart, or on good ol' Charlie
Brown, would produce nothing more than the world's darkest
"Peanuts perplex":

Also, we have no intention of attempting to nail down the specific intentions of Mr. Schulz. Attempts at passing these kinds of judgment are, in the last analysis, attempts to "play God"—a role which has never proved *too* popular with the heavenly powers and which, therefore, can lead to all kinds of embarrassing situations:

"Therefore do not pronounce judgment before the time," advises St. Paul. For it is only God who knows "the purposes of the heart" (1 Cor. 4:5). But even if the actual intentions of the artist *could* be finally known, this should not limit the vision of the interpreter. Art, just as T. S. Eliot has said of a poem, "is not just either what the poet 'planned' or what the reader conceives, nor is its 'use' restricted wholly to what the author intended or to what it actually does for readers."[27] According to Paul, even those who spoke in tongues were

often not aware of the meaning of their strange speech, and therefore they themselves looked to interpreters for "edification" (1 Cor.
14:13).

Our approach to *Peanuts*, then, will not be one of "reading *into*"
but of "reading *out of*"; our concern will not be so much in trying to
say what Mr. Schulz has actually put *into* his cartoons, as in saying
what has come *out of* his cartoons to us. Confession, or witness, is
the basis of a Christian interpretation of art as it is the basis of a
Christian interpretation of anything. It just may be, however, if an
interpretation should seem to account coherently for all or most of
the puzzle's pieces, that the interpreter's intuition has coincided
exactly with the artist's vision. But still there is no way of knowing
for sure. *This* the reader must decide for himself.

Occasionally we run into people who do not care to have their
Peanuts "salted"—nor do they care for salt with any other form of
art. "Why can't you theologians just let us enjoy these things?" is
their plea. Well said! We are certainly not interested in killing
anyone's joy—quite the contrary! We wish them continued and
more abundant joy! We would only wish to suggest, however, that
the defenders of such a radical distinction or separation of Church
and art *first* do the artist no favor by suggesting that his art is
capable of no other purpose than satisfying our cravings for enjoy-
ment. Granted the latter is a high calling. But to say that art *can*
not nor *should* not nor *does* not do more than this is to sell the
artist far short of the important role he has always played in shaping
men's lives. And as Eliot has said, in words applicable for all artists,
"... the author, whatever his conscious intentions in writing, in
practice recognizes no such distinctions. The author of a work of
imagination is trying to affect us wholly, as human beings, whether
he knows it or not; and we are affected by it, as human beings,
whether we intend to be or not."[28]

Second, such a desire for the separation of the Church and the
arts betrays the quality of faith—just as all judgments of art will—
behind such an objection: it is a "faith" so little that it cannot conceive of itself except as existing in some tiny, closed compartment; a
faith that does not have relevance to *all* of life, and hence is no

faith at all, but only a small hole large enough at best for the head of
a human ostrich. A faith that can find no significant meaning in
art and laughter, in the tragic as well as in the hilariously comic, is
a faith that will find no joy in life itself. "By faith we understand
that the world was created by the word of God, so that what is seen
was made out of things which do not appear" (Heb. 11:3). If the
Church fails to use the divine imagination given to it, to see the unseen, to see "sermons in stones and good in everything," to see "that
all that passes to corruption is a parable,"[29] as Karl Barth has put it,
it will constantly be embarrassed by a world capable of far more
imagination than the Church itself.

The heart is deceitful above all things, and desperately corrupt;
who can understand it?

—*Jeremiah 17:9*

All have sinned and fall short of the glory of God.

—*Romans 3:23*

It never fails. Just *hint* that some of their troubles might be with
themselves, and they get mad at you!

—*Snoopy*

II. "The Whole Trouble": Original Sin

Although "sin" may not be a very original topic, it is nevertheless
Original Sin we now want to discuss. The original sinfulness of man
—all men—is almost taken for granted by the New Testament; it is
the *background* for almost everything the New Testament says.
Christ himself usually seemed to presuppose this view of human
nature. For instance, Christ was addressing every one of the entire
"multitude" when he said in the Sermon on the Mount, "If you then,
who are evil, know how to give good gifts to your children . . .," and
so on (Matt. 7:11). As Karl Barth has put it, "Just because Christ
is born, we have to regard the world as lost in the sight of God."[1]
For unless the entire world of man is hopelessly mired in the depths
of a predicament from which there is *no* possible escape or salvation,
then it is really unnecessary for a "Savior of the world" to come into
the world. "We are convinced that one has died for all," says St.
Paul; "therefore all have died" (2 Cor. 5:14). This is why the New
Testament can say that "Jesus did not trust himself to them, because
he knew all men and needed no one to bear witness of man; for he
himself knew what was in man" (John 2:24). And "what was in
man," according to Christ?

> Hear me, all of you, and understand: there is nothing outside a
> man which by going into him can defile him. . . . What comes out
> of a man is what defiles a man. For from within, out of the heart
> of man, come evil thoughts, fornication, theft, murder, adultery,
> coveting, wickedness, deceit, licentiousness, envy, slander, pride,
> foolishness. All these evil things come from within, and they
> defile a man (Mark 7:14-15, 20-23).

"Hear me, all of you, and understand," pleaded Christ with what
may have been a touch of impatience. For man's naturally hard

heart is not only the final barrier Christ's gospel has for being heard
and understood, as we attempted to point out in the last chapter, but
this *basic sinfulness* also explains why men will constantly *disclaim*
their own basic sinfulness—or, in the case of the Church, will constantly *forget* it. Wrote Luther: "So great is the corruption and
blindness of human nature that it does not see or sense the greatness
of sin"[2]—or, we might add, does not see or sense "the corruption and
blindness of human nature." Lucy sums up this "whole trouble"
this way:

But Lucy is not such a good listener either. In another cartoon she
tells Charlie Brown, "The whole trouble with you is you don't understand the meaning of life!" "Do *you* understand the meaning of

life?" he asks her. Her reply: "We're not talking about me, we're talking about you!"

The doctrine of Original Sin is a theme constantly being dramatized in *Peanuts*. And as Lucy asks Charlie Brown, after demonstrating to him how his pebble-like virtues are no match for the boulder representing his "countless faults," "Don't you think you're lucky to have me around to point up these things in such a graphic manner?" Indeed we are lucky! For as Hume maintained, one of the best ways of putting new flesh onto the bones of old and misunderstood creeds is precisely to point up these things in a graphic manner.[3] Therefore, in such a manner we shall proceed.

First of all, the doctrine of Original Sin (including the Garden of Eden story) is not so much concerned with *how* the human predicament got the way it is, as it is concerned to show *what* the human predicament is. And what is the "human predicament"? It is that each one of us, every man born of a woman, is *born* under the *curse* of sin ("A curse comes to being/As a child is formed"[4]), that we all have our own personal *origins* in sin, that we all *originate* this way in life—and hence the term *"Origin-al Sin."* (This is also why some churches call Original Sin, "Birth-Sin.") But this sinfulness does not necessarily manifest itself in meanness or hatefulness; it can often show up in our consciousness as a type of "nameless woe":

Christ made it perfectly clear that it was simply not enough for
one to be born only *once* in a lifetime—"unless one is born anew,
he cannot see the kingdom of God." For "that which is born of the
flesh is flesh, and that which is born of the Spirit is spirit" (John
3:3, 6). Thus "the day of one's birth" has great significance throughout the Bible. As the origin of one's destiny for good or for ill, the

birthday is either "blessed" or "cursed." "So much in this world depends upon who gets born first!" complains Linus when he is left out in the rain by his older sister, Lucy, on the basis of her getting to the umbrella first. Hence Christ could say, "woe to that man by whom the Son of man is betrayed! good were it for that man if he had never been born" (Mark 14:21, K.J.V.).

It is important to make clear that Original Sin does not refer to any immoral acts or evil deeds we have ever done. It is pointing to something much *deeper* than specific deeds, because it refers to the basic origin or motive behind *everything* we *always* do. In other words, we are not sinners because we "occasionally sin," but we "sin occasionally" because we are *always* sinners. "Sins" is only *one* of the ways in which *sin* can manifest itself. "The whole trouble," then, lies in *who we are—basically,* or to begin with:

The doctrine of Original Sin also means that man's *will* is in total and complete bondage to sin. As an example of a doctrinal expression of this view, *The Book of Common Prayer* puts it this way:

> The condition of Man after the fall of Adam is such, that he cannot turn and prepare himself, by his own natural strength and good works, to faith, and calling upon God. Wherefore we have no power to do good works pleasant and acceptable to God, without the grace of God by Christ preventing us, that we may have a good will, and working with us, when we have that good will ("Articles of Religion," X).

But probably the most famous biblical expression for the captivity of man's will in sin is found in Romans, where the "wretched" St. Paul writes:

> I do not understand my own actions. For I do not do what I want, but I do the very thing I hate. . . . For I know that nothing good dwells within me, that is, in my flesh. I can will what is right, but I cannot do it. . . . For I delight in the law of God, in my inmost self, but I see in my members another law at war with the law of my mind and making me captive to the law of sin which dwells in my members. Wretched man that I am! Who will deliver me from this body of death? (Rom. 7:15, 18, 22-24).

In the following cartoon, Lucy almost manages to out-Paul Paul at this point by not only saying the same thing in so many words, but she also is again able "to point up" the entire business in her well-known "graphic manner"—this time to the "wretched" Linus:

And what does St. Paul mean when he says, "I can will what is right, but I cannot do it"? Probably something like this:

And what does St. Paul mean when he says, "I do not understand my own actions"? Probably something like what Linus says when Lucy asks him why he tore the cover off her comic magazine: "I don't know. I really don't know. Why do I do stupid things? Why don't I think? What's the matter with me? Where's my sense of responsibility? Then I ask myself, am I really responsible? Is it really my fault when I do something wrong? Must I answer for my mistakes?" *POW!*—She lets him have it with all the wrath of an angry God impatient with a will trapped in the paralysis of analysis. "Her kind never worries about these things!" observes the flattened Linus.

The captivity of man's will is most often dramatized in *Peanuts* just as it is most often dramatized in men's lives—by the significant *change* that never takes place. In talking about the egotism and brutality of children, Schulz has said, "We grown-ups don't change so much, except on the surface, because we get along better that way."[5] J. D. Salinger is making the same point in *Franny and Zooey* when he has Zooey tell his sister:

> And don't tell me again that you were ten years old. Your age has nothing to do with what I am talking about. There are no big *changes* between ten and twenty—or ten and eighty, for that matter. You *still* can't love a Jesus as much as you'd like to who did and said a couple of things he was at least reported to have said or done—and you know it.[6]

The inability of the *Peanuts* kids to produce any radical change for the better in themselves—or in each other—is a constant *Peanuts* theme. When Charlie Brown feels he has lost the respect of his little sister, Sally, because he cowardly failed to protect her from a playground bully, Linus tries to cheer him up by asking if he did not wish he "had it all to do over." But Charlie Brown can only reply, "No, I'd probably do the same thing." When Charlie Brown, on the other hand, tries to cheer up the blanket-loving Linus, who is about to receive a visit from his "blanket-hating grandma," he tells Linus that "maybe she has calmed down since the last time she was here." "Maybe the moon will fall out of the sky!" responds Linus with what later proves to be well-founded skepticism. Lucy's answer to

Charlie Brown when he mentions that she is wearing her "crabby face again," is "There's nothing wrong with being crabby! I'm proud of being crabby! The crabby little girls of today are the crabby old women of tomorrow!!" But later when Lucy does make an honest effort "to be nicer to people," her girl friend Patty tells her: "You'll never be able to change! You'll always be a crabby little girl! You were born crabby, and you're going to stay crabby! Don't think you're going to change because you're not!" "Suddenly I feel a great sense of relief!" responds Lucy, who was finding it difficult not being herself anyway. The classic *Peanuts* commentary on this rather pessimistic view of human nature is the running gag every year when Charlie Brown's courageous views on man's freedom and goodness are invariably brought back to earth by Lucy:

Lucy's "bonded word," then, sounds more like what theologians have called "the bondage of the will"; and Charlie Brown sounds very much like a follower of Pelagius, who also was "accustomed . . . to call attention to the capacity and character of human nature and to show what it is able to accomplish."[7] However, Pelagianism itself was brought down to earth by being condemned as heresy at the third General Council in Ephesus in 431. But, as Pascal once complained, the Church will always have its share of Pelagians. One elderly latter-day pillar of the Church, after having the doctrine of Original Sin explained to her, is said to have exclaimed angrily, "Well, if all of us really are as bad off as all that, then God help us!" In the case of Pelagianism, it is *often* difficult to know whether to weep or to laugh.

And so "I have already charged that all men . . . are under the power of sin" (Rom. 3:9); we are all thrown into life, or wake up, "under a curse" (Gal. 3:10). As in the case of the man born blind (John 9), this situation is not "our fault" nor the fault of our parents. "The state in which we find ourselves is sinful, quite independent of guilt,"[8] as Kafka put it. We are cursed simply because we all have the birth defect of lacking the one thing needful—faith in our creator. No one makes his entrance in the world with built-in faith, or comes on the scene worshiping God. "What! Did the word of God originate with you . . . ?" (1 Cor. 14:36). But even though "the divine promise of grace is not a light that is born in us,"[9] we are never immediately aware or conscious of this inward darkness because of its depth inside us. As natural men we wake up in life with faith in the natural and with a feeling of well-being; as men of the world we come into the world feeling that both life and we personally are basically good. It is not until we *really* wake up that we discover the precariousness of our situation: we have waked up "in the doghouse" with powers much higher than ourselves. "Even so we, when we were children, were in bondage under the elements of the world" (Gal. 4:3, K.J.V.):

This situation is also what the New Testament means by being "under the law." The law teaches us that we are not as good or as God-like as we thought we were. It does this by placing us in a situation in which we *must*—and yet in which we *cannot*—help ourselves. Hence Paul could say, "I was once alive apart from the law, but when the commandment came, sin revived and I died" (Rom. 7:9). "For the mind that is set on the flesh . . . does not submit to God's law, indeed it cannot" (Rom. 8:7).

How do we get out of this doghouse that we can suddenly find ourselves trapped in? Or, as Christ put it, "How can Satan cast out Satan?" (Mark 3:23). Answer: "it depends not upon man's will or exertion, but upon God's mercy" (Rom. 9:16). In other words "it is by grace, it is no longer on the basis of works; otherwise grace would no longer be grace" (Rom. 11:6). This is why God's mercy has often been called or thought of as *"irresistible* grace." Our own

captive wills are overcome by a stronger will, by "something we just can't resist." And this is precisely how the doomed Snoopy is finally "saved." Charlie Brown calls the "humane society," which recommends "coaxing him out with his favorite food—something he just can't resist." Thus Snoopy is "Saved by a pizza!" For the icicle falls and demolishes his doghouse immediately after he "zooms out" to the food he cannot resist.

Therefore in the New Testament it is not the work of a man's *hands,* but only the faith in Christ of a man's *heart,* or one's "hunger for righteousness," that can save or satisfy a man. And because man's naturally proud heart can only be bent toward God *by* God, faith is never a basis for "boasting," whereas the works of a man's own hands can be.

Then what becomes of our boasting? It is excluded. On what principle? On the principle of works? No, but on the principle of faith. For we hold that a man is justified by faith apart from works of law (Rom. 3:27-28).

For no matter how many good works or righteous deeds a person may have done throughout a *lifetime,* they are all for *nothing,* as far as his own final satisfaction is concerned, if they have been done for the wrong reasons—or, to put it metaphorically, if they have been done with "dirty hands." From the attempts of Pontius Pilate or Lady Macbeth to cleanse their guilty hands, to the modern play *Dirty Hands* by Sartre, dirty hands have often been used by writers as an outward sign of an inward disgrace. Therefore, "cleanse your hands, you sinners, and purify your hearts. . . . Humble yourselves before the Lord and he will exalt you. . . . As it is, you boast in your arrogance. All such boasting is evil" (James 4:8, 10, 16).

We can laugh at Linus because he gets stopped cold before he gets started down this particular path. Unfortunately however this is not always the case. Take for instance the lament of the great "king over Israel" of Ecclesiastes, "the Preacher," as he neared the end of his life: "Then I considered all that my hands had done and the toil I had spent in doing it, and behold, all was vanity and a striving after wind, and there was nothing to be gained under the sun" (Eccles. 2:11).

Man's sinful nature, from which he never escapes, is not only the cause for every man and every generation having to learn the truth for themselves from scratch, but it is also the cause of the stubbornly sluggish memories of those who *have* learned the truth—the Church. Thus the admonition to "Remember!" is thrust again and again throughout the Bible at God's elected people. For it is the unfortunate natural tendency of even the *justified* sinner to forget his own personal encounter with God and to want to exchange the natural for the "supernatural," the seen for the unseen, knowledge for faith, the controllable for the uncontrollable, the verifiable for the unverifiable, the creature for the creator, the visible authority for the invisible authority. To insure its remembrance of its God—both God as he was known in history as Jesus, and is subsequently known in men's hearts in and through Jesus in the person of the Holy Spirit—to insure this remembrance, the Church has various holy "signposts": the *sacraments* ("Do this in remembrance of me," Luke 22:19) ; *Scripture* ("You search the scriptures, because you think that in them you have eternal life; and it is they that bear witness to me," John 5:39) ; and the *churches* (". . . you shall be my witnesses in Jerusalem and in all Judea and Samaria and to the end of the earth," Acts 1:8), to name the most important signposts. "God is spirit, and those who worship him must worship in spirit and truth" (John 4:24). Therefore, difficulty always arises for the Church when it forgets that the spirit blows where it wills (John 3:8) and that "No man has power to retain the spirit" (Eccles. 8:8). For then the Church invariably seeks to substitute *for* God a visible signpost pointing *to* God. And thus Scripture, the *report* of the Word of God, can become *the* Word of God; a certain sacramental channel of

God's grace can become *the* channel of grace; a particular church can become *the* church. Hence men constantly have the tendency when pointing to the Church to say it is "on this mountain" or "in Jerusalem" (John 4:21) or to "say, 'Lo, here it is!' or 'There!'" forgetting that Christ insisted quite emphatically that "the kingdom of God is within you" (Luke 17:21). Mr. Schulz has said:

> I am a trifle odd, perhaps, in my feeling about these things, but I believe that one cannot, so to speak, "go" to church. How can you go to something that you are already a part of? If you are a Christian, you *are* the church.[10]

At any rate, there are undoubtedly many ways of expressing this view, and perhaps the following cartoon is one of them:

All of us, "the human race," to quote John Henry Newman, "is implicated in some terrible aboriginal calamity."[11] And even though the doctrine of Original Sin may be *"The* Doctrine which emerges from all honest study of history,"[12] it is nevertheless·an article of belief. "Original Sin is foolishness to men, but it is admitted to be such," said Pascal. "And how should it be perceived by his reason, since it is a thing against reason, and since reason, far from finding it out by her own ways, is averse to it when it is presented to her?"[13] Or, as Linus has put it, "How can you do 'new math' problems with an 'old math' mind?" Just as it is only in belief, or personal experience, that Christ can become Christ "for me," it is only in belief that the world can be known to be filled with hatred—"for me."

"All men naturally hate one another. They employ lust as far as possible in the service of the public weal."[14] This is the same view

that prompted Augustine to say that the glorious virtues of the good pagans were no more than splendid vices, and brought Calvin to insist that any government based on this more realist appraisal of man's nature would have greater chance of success than some Utopian society based on an "ideal" man:

> The vice or imperfection of men therefore renders it safer and more tolerable for the government to be in the hands of many, that they may afford each other mutual assistance and admonition, and that if any one arrogate to himself more than is right, the many may act as censors and masters to restrain his ambition.[15]

For men will even forget their natural enmity, and co-operate—as long as they believe helping each other will serve their own purposes:

The LORD looks down from heaven upon the children of men, to see if there are any that act wisely, that seek after God. They have all gone astray, they are all alike corrupt; there is none that does good, no, not one (Ps. 14:2-3).

The "children of men" of the preceding psalm could be well represented by the children of *Peanuts,* for in both cases *all* seem to have "gone astray." Even the lovable and long-suffering Charlie Brown, as Schulz has said of him, "never does anything mean, but he is weak, vain and very vulnerable.... And aren't all kids egotists?" Schulz asks. "And brutal? Children are caricatures of adults."[16] Indeed Mr. Schulz had originally planned to call his strip *Li'l Folks,* and evidently was quite disappointed with the "terrible insignificance" of the "Peanuts" title, when the strip was renamed by a cartoon syndicate.[17]

Children can be a good symbol for the original sinfulness of man since all men originate as children *and* as sinners. "Behold, I was brought forth in iniquity, and in sin did my mother conceive me" (Ps. 51:5). For this reason the children of *Peanuts* can be seen as a sort of comic counterpart to the kind of children found in William Golding's terrifying tract of the times, *Lord of the Flies.* Golding's children, along with an increasing number of young people in modern literature, help us to see that unaccommodated man—left completely free to be himself, to do what comes naturally, without gospel and in spite of law—is a savage. Golding puts it this way in commenting on his book:

The theme is an attempt to trace the defects of society back to the defects of human nature. The moral is that the shape of a society must depend on the ethical nature of the individual and not on any political system however apparently logical or respectable. The whole book is symbolic in nature except the rescue in the end where adult life appears dignified and capable, but in reality enmeshed in the same evil as the symbolic life of the children on the island. The officer, having interrupted a man-hunt, prepares to take the children off the island in a cruiser which will presently be hunting its enemy in the same implacable way. And who will rescue the adult and his cruiser?[18]

Golding's analogy thus moves from children to adults to nations; with precisely the same results, it moves precisely like this:

Seeing the infant as a sinner, however, probably never has been nor will be a popular point of view. It may be, therefore, that the modern "cult of the child," which holds to the child's "original innocence," is partly a reaction against the doctrine of Original Sin. "Those who hold that human nature is essentially good ('unfallen') and corrupted only by society," writes H. A. Grunwald, "regard the child as an unspoiled bundle of life which 'goes wrong' mostly because of bad things happening in the 'environment.'"[19] Whenever they can, even the youngest *Peanuts* children are crafty enough to take advantage of this point of view:

Once when Linus breaks a table lamp at home while chasing a toy airplane, Lucy tells him, "Ha! Now, you've done it! And you've got no one to blame it on but yourself!" After reflecting a moment Linus suggests, "Maybe I could blame it on society!" Christ used children as an analogy for the *attitude*—rather than the *basis* for the attitude—of trust and humility that men must assume before they can *become* "children of God." Thus men are to "turn and become like children"—rather than to remain or be children (Matt. 18:3). "This means that it is not the children of the flesh who are the children of God, but the children of the promise are reckoned as descendents" (Rom. 9:8). Or, as St. John put it, "to all who ... believed in his name, he gave power to become children of God; who were born, not of blood nor of the will of the flesh nor of the will of man, but of God" (John 1:12, 13). The same unsentimental view of children has not only prompted Mr. Schulz to say, "Maybe

I have the cruelest strip going," but it has also prompted angry letters from readers protesting this "cruelty."[20] *Peanuts,* however, only protests in turn against such sentimentality. One day, for example, after being laughed out of the presence of his boyfriends, Charlie Brown proceeds down the sidewalk:

As Grunwald points out, the myth of the innocent child strongly resembles the myth of the noble savage—savage perhaps, but not too noble. Even much of modern depth psychology has come to St. Augustine's conclusion that the so-called innocence of children is more a matter of weakness of limb than purity of heart. Therefore, it is probably best that we still do not give children real guns to play with.

"Among these we all once lived in the passions of our flesh, following the desires of body and mind, and so we were by nature children of wrath, like the rest of mankind" (Eph. 2:3). Grunwald concludes that "the view of unfallen human nature is shallow and illusory," and that "we have made fools of ourselves in the cult of the child and in its origin, which is really the cult of man; and yet one can still feel that the child has a special place in human emotions."[21] Indeed the child does have this special place; for it comes into the world completely unaware of, and not responsible for, the fallenness of the race into which it nevertheless is thrust as also fallen. Thus Original Sin is often thought of as "inherited guilt." "It's always the children who suffer for the sins of the mother and father!" complains Linus in one cartoon; "It's the children who are always the victims of sin and dishonor," agrees Charlie Brown in another. "For I the LORD your God am a jealous God, visiting the iniquity of the fathers upon the children to the third and fourth generation of those who hate me," echoes a familiar Old Testament refrain (Exod. 20:5; Deut. 5:9). This kind of "original innocence" of children, as Lucy says of it, "doesn't solve anything, but it makes us all feel better." But the innocence of the *Peanuts* kids is never an innocence of shallow and sinless "cuteness"; it is always an innocence with biblical or metaphysical overtones, an innocence of being "innocent but not too well informed," as Schulz has said of Linus.

There are, of course, many people who do not believe in the doctrine of Original Sin. They feel, like Linus, that deep down inside of his heart of hearts man really is basically good in spite of everything, and that therefore the entire world in general is surely getting better and better. This is the stubborn faith that men have in themselves, and it is often a touching and courageous faith to behold. Its greatest weakness, however, is that even though it gives us a great dream or hope for what may be coming, it never quite makes sense out of what honestly *is—now*. And dreams based only on dreams, rather than on reality, will be as disastrous for the future as they are unsatisfying for the present.

"There is nothing on earth," said Pascal, "that does not show either the wretchedness of man, or the mercy of God; either the weakness of man without God, or the strength of man with God."[22] But regardless of how completely the doctrine of Original Sin may make sense to some observers, this universal hardness of heart will never really be overcome or understood by an appeal to man's mind, or by "making sense." It can only be overcome by a change in the heart itself.

There is a way which seems right to a man, but its end is the way to death. Even in laughter the heart is sad, and the end of joy is grief.

—*Proverbs 14:12-13*

Little children, keep yourselves from idols.

—*1 John 5:21*

For although there may be so-called gods in heaven or on earth—as indeed there are many "gods" and many "lords"—yet for us there is one God, the Father, from whom are all things and for whom we exist, and one Lord, Jesus Christ, through whom are all things and through whom we exist.

—*1 Corinthians 8:5-6*

I never said I *worship* Miss Othmar. I just said that I'm very fond of the ground on which she walks!

—*Linus*

III. The Wages of Sin Is "Aaaughh!"

Calvin once said that the human mind is a permanent factory of idols. And what is an "idol"? As Luther put it, "Trust and faith of the heart alone make both God and idol. . . . Whatever then thy heart clings to and relies upon, that is properly thy God."[1] "For where your treasure is"—where the center of your existence is, whatever is most important in life for you, that gives meaning, hope, order, and direction to your life—"there will your heart be also" (Matt. 6:21). This means that everyone has some kind of "god" or "faith" or "belief"; there are no "atheists"—a word never found in the Bible. Trying to live without a god, without some kind of ultimate concern in life, is like trying to play a baseball game without a home plate—it can not be done. Mr. Schulz has told us that Linus' blanket "is a symbol of things we cling to." But what about Linus' "blanket-hating Grandma"? According to Lucy, "She believes children should be taught self-denial; she believes in discipline; she believes in moral fiber." According to Linus, "She believes in butting into other people's business!!" But is this grandmother free from "things we cling to"? Not according to Mr. Schulz: "Not long ago I had Linus' blanket-hating grandmother come to his house for a visit. She tried to get him to give up his propensity for the blanket; so he threw up to her the fact that she was drinking 32 cups of coffee a day!"[2] Finally, all of us—even young people—have some one

thing we cling to, some joy above all others, some "cause" that causes
us to go on living in the particular ways we live:

Furthermore, it is possible to have only *one* "god" at a time, only
one *supreme* value—unless of course one is genuinely "two," a real
"dual personality." Secondary values can be many, but "No one can
serve two masters; for either he will hate the one and love the
other, or he will be devoted to the one and despise the other. You
cannot serve God and mammon" (Matt. 6:24):

"If mankind be itself God, the appearance of the idol is then inevitable."[3] And so it is that the original sinfulness of men usually manifests itself, is garnered up, comes to a head in a more or less clearly defined idolatry of one kind or another. As far as the Bible is concerned there are only two *kinds* of gods available to man—the *real* one and the *phony* one, but there are multitudinous variations of the phony god, ranging from the intellectually sublime to the childishly ridiculous—and vice versa. All phony gods, however, have one thing in common: it kills your soul to worship one of them. It is your god, you love it, you are a slave to it, and you will stick with it to the bitter end come hell or high water.

But this is unfortunate. For in the biblical view of idolatry the end necessarily will be bitter, and indeed will involve a type of hell, as all phony gods inevitably will prove to be the cruelest possible

taskmasters. This is all St. Paul meant when he said, "the wages of
sin is death" (Rom. 6:23). "Sin" for Paul meant no more or no
less than worshiping any other god than the God who is met only
in and through Jesus Christ. And by "death" Paul did not mean
physical death; but he meant a type of spiritual death, a living
death, a fate far worse than death, a death which man can actually
experience as no less than hell during his lifetime, and hence a death
from which man can actually be "saved" here and now. For the wages
of sin *is* death—now. Or, to paraphrase Paul's famous statement,
the result of idolatry is "a rudely clobbered belief" (Linus); and "in
all this world there is nothing more upsetting than the clobbering of
a cherished belief" (Charlie Brown).

All the *Peanuts* kids are guilty of this kind of sin, of serving a false
god; and all receive their inevitable wages in this kind of emotional
clobbering.

This theme is so constant in *Peanuts* that the strip truly can
be seen as a kind of "child's garden of reverses." Take Linus for
instance. His blanket (this "portable security," this source of "mental
therapy," this "spiritual blotter" soaking up "fears and frustra-
tions"!) is obviously intended to cover a multitude of sins for him,
but it inevitably turns out to be only a drag, as it is surely the world's
longest and most vulnerable Achilles' heel. One might wonder why
he continues to suffer for it so; but, as he says, it is all he has: "Only
one yard of outing flannel stands between me and a nervous breakdown!" And if there should be any doubt in the reader's mind that
such an idol can actually mean the difference between being *lost* or
saved, the following cartoon should remove any question:

Perhaps Linus will outgrow his blanket? "What are you going to do when you get too old to drag it around?" Charlie Brown asks him. "Who knows?" he replies. "I've been thinking seriously of having it made over into a sport coat!" No one can part with one's *god* until one *has* to, until there is no part of it left to cling to. A *god*, by definition, is all we have "to keep us going," as Linus has put it. Charlie Brown is kept going by his desire to win, but has yet to win anything, whether in terms of friends, baseball games, or kite-flying contests between him and his unco-operative kites. Schroeder, who idolizes Beethoven, has been known to die a thousand deaths on such occasions as forgetting his hero's birthday. Even Lucy, the last of the great rugged individualists, and who has been called everything from a fascist to a pint-sized Lucifer (she *is* a little devil at times), has a shrine before which she stands or falls. And she has fallen—for Schroeder:

As a matter of fact, this answer is not far from *the* answer: "Take heed to yourselves, lest you forget the covenant of the LORD your God, which he made with you, and make a graven image in the form of anything which the LORD your God has forbidden you. For the LORD your God is a devouring fire, a jealous God" (Deut. 4:23-24). To put it another way, you shall "fall in love" with no other god. For it is not until we seek *first* the Kingdom of God and *his* righteousness that all the Schroeders of our lives can then find satisfactory places in our lives.

But *Peanuts* manages to demonstrate the hazards of worshiping deities that are far more familiar than blankets, winning, Beethoven, or Schroeder. There is for instance the belief we can have in ourselves, or in our own abilities—the well-known "power of positive thinking":

As we have seen, faith in one's own abilities is what the New Testament is getting at when it talks of "law" or "works." Therefore, as far as the New Testament is concerned, it is not by law or ordinances or even by "working a little harder" that man can break through the hardness of heart, or "the dividing wall of hostility," existing between man and man. The answer to this problem can be found only in Christ, as expressed in this way:

For [Christ] is our peace, who has made us both one, and has broken down the dividing wall of hostility, by abolishing in his flesh the law of commandments and ordinances, that he might create in himself one new man in place of the two, so making peace (Eph. 2:14-15).

In the following cartoon this problem of "the dividing wall of hostility," is expressed in such a way as also to suggest the answer given above:

But if one cannot save oneself by believing in one's own abilities or by working a little harder, perhaps one can find help in *friends.* For after all, what are friends for if not to help us find just that extra little bit of strength we need, which comes in knowing we are not alone?

Poor Charlie Brown! The psalmist surely must have had him in mind when he wrote, "Insults have broken my heart, so that I am in despair. I looked for pity, but there was none and for comforters, but I found none" (Ps. 69:20). Indeed the psalmist *could* have had "Charlie Brown" in mind. For Charlie Brown, with his globe-like head (Lucy has used it as a globe several times) and his T-shirt of thorns, can be seen as a sort of twentieth-century representation of Everyman. We love him just as misery loves company; for usually he is just as miserable as most of mankind is. "An interviewer once

wrote that one of my characters, Charlie Brown, mirrors some of my
own childhood troubles," comments Schulz. "That may be true, but
he is also a reflection of the troubles of millions of others—or so I
gather from those who write me."[4] Charlie seeks for hope in the
same kind of human love we all look to, and for this reason his
hopelessness always has a touch of the infinite about it. For "in
human love there is never such a thing as victory: only a few minor
tactical successes before the final defeat of death or indifference," as
Graham Greene wrote in *The Heart of the Matter* (which is, in-
cidentally, one of the books listed by Schulz as being important in
shaping his "vocational attitude and philosophy of life"[5]).

But the psalmist anticipated the answer as well as the problem:

It is better to take refuge in the LORD than to put confidence in man. It is better to take refuge in the LORD than to put confidence in princes (Ps. 118:8-9).

Indeed, as an illustrated chronicle of contemporary heresies, *Peanuts* seems to run the gamut. For instance, the modern road to salvation via "psychiatric help" (" 5¢—The Doctor is IN") often comes in for a lampooning. "I helped you a lot! I pointed out all of your faults! I proved to you that psychiatry is an exact science!" Dr. Lucy tells Charlie Brown. "An *exact science?!*" he shouts in disbelief. "Yes, you owe me exactly one hundred and forty-three dollars!" Dr. Lucy is also a great advocate of a position sounding suspiciously similar to much modern existential philosophy. She seems to be acquainted with its terminology as well as its circular reasoning:

Linus has his own "distinct philosophy" that nevertheless seems to have got around somehow. It is called: "No problem is so big or so complicated that it can't be run away from!" Charlie Brown, however, has trouble understanding some of its finer points:

A variation on the "running" cult is the attempt of modern man to lose himself in a passionless and riskless objectivity of science or the academic. In this case, life is not a hot or even cold *experience,* but merely an "interesting" lukewarm *experiment,* fully deserving to be spewed out of God's mouth (Rev. 3:16). Said Kierkegaard:

> It is a torture to the soul to note the callous incorrigibility with which a human being can resort to wherever he thinks there is some truth to be had, for the sole purpose of learning to expound it, so that his music box may add this piece to its repertoire; but as for doing anything about it, the thing never even occurs to him.[6]

Schulz says the same thing this way:

In *Peanuts* religious heresy seems to be represented by the "Great Pumpkin," Linus' substitute for Santa Claus. Linus believes ("with every fiber of his being") that every year "on Halloween night the 'Great Pumpkin' rises up out of the pumpkin patch and brings toys to all the good little children in the world!" "You're crazy!" Charlie Brown tells him. "All right," replies Linus, "so you believe in Santa Claus, and I'll believe in the 'Great Pumpkin.' The way I see it, it doesn't matter what you believe just so you're sincere!" Furthermore, the "Great Pumpkin" will only appear in "the pumpkin patch that he thinks is the most sincere." Over and over, Schulz seems to be saying that *sincerity* is no more a guarantee of truth than it is a guarantee of success. "How can we lose when we're so sincere?" laments Charlie Brown after his baseball team loses another game—

this one "one hundred and eighty-four to nothing!" Again, Schulz seems to be in agreement with Kierkegaard, who said, "Evil, mediocrity, is never so dangerous as when it is dressed up as 'sincerity'. "[7] The "Great Pumpkin," then, may be symbolic of popular religious sentiment, which currently seems to have more "faith in faith," or faith in "sincerity," than faith in anything in particular.[8] At any rate, the cult of the "Great Pumpkin" is surely "religious," as also is its rival, the Santa Claus sect. When Charlie Brown is asked if he believes there really *is* a Santa Claus, he replies, "I refuse to get involved in a theological discussion." Linus admits he has been "a victim of false doctrine" after the "Great Pumpkin" fails to show up for the umpteenth consecutive time. At this point Linus writes a book on his "experiences with the 'Great Pumpkin.' " "I call it," he says of his book, *"My Belief Was Rudely Clobbered."* Later, after an argument with Linus on the merits of the "Great Pumpkin" compared with Santa Claus, Charlie Brown concludes, "We are obviously separated by denominational differences." These differences are interesting. For as the "Great Pumpkin" seems indeed to represent "false doctrine," the ideas surrounding Santa Claus seem to be "doctrinally" sound. For instance, the attitude Linus has toward Santa Claus is the same attitude many Christians have toward God: they feel that by obeying his "law," God then *owes* them something. Again, this means that the gift of God is not a gift, that "grace is not grace," but a *reward* for man's own righteousness —and hence an occasion for an inevitable human pride:

These discussions centering around Santa Claus often take on theological proportions. For instance, if we read "God" for "Santa Claus" in the following cartoon, Shermy's argument then takes the form of a familiar argument for complete freedom in morality:

Shermy is *right* in that God's love is *finally* triumphant over man, "no matter *how* man acts"; *wrong* in that there is no way of really knowing this apart from faith in—and hence obedience to—God *now*. So Shermy is only "hoping to goodness"; and as Linus once remarked, " 'Hoping to goodness' is not theologically sound." The disobedient man is foolish to "presume upon the riches of [God's] kindness and forbearance and patience" (Rom. 2:4). For in the meantime, the wages of sin *is* death, hell—*now*. Thus:

> Woe unto you, scribes and Pharisees, hypocrites! for ye . . . outwardly appear righteous unto men, but within ye are full of hypocrisy and iniquity. . . . ye generation of vipers, how can ye escape the damnation of hell? . . . O Jerusalem, Jerusalem, thou that killest the prophets . . . how often would I have gathered thy children together, even as a hen gathereth her chickens under her wings, and ye would not! (Matt. 23:27-28, 33, 37, K.J.V.).

It is important to make clear that the dreadful "sickness unto death," or "hell," that is the inevitable accompaniment of sin, does not always wait to occur with the collapse of particular deities. Often this bottomless fear rises into our consciousness as a type of nameless anxiety or fear of "nothingness"—or fear of *everything*. And since there is no way of dealing with such an indefinable and irrational dread, this nameless woe is usually far more horrible than the anxiety accompanying the collapse of any particular "strange god." Such anxiety is bottomless and indefinable just because the very foundation of our lives, the very basis from which *everything* was heretofore defined and dealt with, has *itself* collapsed, has become radically questionable and without any apparent reason. Originally sin-full, we are brought into the world as "hollow men"; and when the hardness of man's heart is finally shattered by God, man finds only *nothing* within. Thus when such a person undergoing this terrible experience has no idea of what is happening to him, there is no greater suffering. But, to use the question Linus asked when he bashed into a tree because of his blanket-obscured vision: "Is there no way out?" Is there no exit, no excuse, no escape from such anxiety? Is there no hiding place from the terrible wrath of God? Only temporary escapes are possible—escapes in which anxiety is pushed back into the depths of the subconscious. But even these escapes are of little help, since the unknown disease is a greater danger than the one of which we are aware; furthermore, consciously or subconsciously, we still remain—apart from God's mercy—"vessels of wrath" (Rom. 9:22).

> Therefore shall evil come upon thee; thou shalt not know from whence it riseth: and mischief shall fall upon thee; thou shalt not be able to put it off: and desolation shall come upon thee suddenly, which thou shalt not know (Isa. 47:11, K.J.V.).

Even the impenetrable "Pig-Pen," with the "dust of countless ages" caked on him an inch thick, is not able to escape these frightening attacks that rise from within:

Some while ago, a feature article on "guilt and anxiety" appearing in *Time* listed the technical names for some of our more particular fears, but explained that these fears are only "neurotic symptoms" acting as defenses against a deeper, far more basic anxiety. Man now rejoices, said *Time*, "that, to some extent, he has been freed from the fear of hell-fire, not realizing that he has instead been condemned to the fear of nothingness."[9] This view, as the article also mentioned, is certainly in agreement with what a great deal of modern theology has been saying. And there are others who would seem to agree. For instance, two months after this article appeared, the following conversation took place in *Peanuts*, using the same technical jargon and—in its own way—driving the same point home, as we can see:

Charlie Brown, who numbers himself "among the walking wounded," and frequently becomes "sick and tired of *everything*," certainly is aware of that *Weltschmerz*, that "world weariness," from which there is no escape: "Can a man hide himself in secret places so that I cannot see him? says the LORD. Do I not fill heaven and earth?" (Jer. 23:24).

Indeed, none of the "Li'l Folks" seem to have escaped from these unknown terrors. Even the youngest of them, Sally Brown, confesses to Dr. Lucy: "My problem is I'm afraid of kindergarten. I don't even know why! I try to reason it out, but I can't! I'm just afraid! I think about it all the time! I'm really afraid!" So Dr. Lucy tells her, "You're no different from anyone else. Five cents, please!" And how is it with the tough-as-nails Dr. Lucy? "I never think about the past," she tells Charlie Brown. "Also, I never worry about the future." "What about the present?" he asks her. *"The present drives me crazy!"* she howls.

The "eternal now" is that present moment in which time seems to stand still while one is paralyzed with terror—and thus hell can and *does* last for an eternity. "How are they brought into desolation, as in a moment! they are utterly consumed with terrors" (Ps. 73:19, κ.ʝ.ᴠ.). T. S. Eliot, in his poem "The Hollow Men," has expressed in the following lines the eternity of darkness that can pass through such moments of doubt and confusion: "Between the idea/And the reality/Between the motion/And the act/Falls the Shadow.... Between the conception/And the creation/Between the emotion/And the response/Falls the Shadow/*Life is very long.... This is the way the world ends/Not with a bang but a whimper.*"[10] "Nothing in life ends with a *pow!*"[11] Schulz has said, echoing the famous last lines of Eliot's poem. And in the following cartoon, Schulz also may have had "The Hollow Men" in mind:

What does Eliot mean when he says, "Life is very long"? Probably the same thing Charlie Brown says when Shermy notices that "winter is on its way. The days are getting shorter": "It's a good thing," Charlie Brown tells him. "The way my days have been going lately, I'd just as soon have them not last too long!" One day, for no apparent reason at all, Lucy suddenly bursts into tears. *"What's the matter, Lucy?* Can I help you?" asks Violet, rushing to Lucy's aid. "No, thank you, Violet (snif). There's nothing you can do," Lucy tells her. "My problems are deep-rooted!" On another occasion Charlie Brown tells Violet, "Gee, I get depressed easily. I don't know what's the matter with me. I just don't know," he says, grasping a small tree for support. "Sometimes I think my soul is full of weeds!" Anton Boisen, a noted psychologist of religion, was pointing to the source of the same deep-rooted weeds when he wrote:

> I believe that man is born subject to human frailties and perversities. Educators may learn much regarding the consequences of errors made in early training, but it is a serious mistake to place all the blame for later maladjustments upon the parents. Even in the best of families and with the best of training, unruly desires deriving from our animal ancestry are likely to manifest themselves. The garden of the heart, even with the best cultivation, is troubled by weeds.[12]

The "child's garden of reverses," *Peanuts,* seems also at times to be an unweeded garden that grows to seed. For here the "weeds of the heart" often seem to be represented by weeds that can be seen, and yet weeds that are nonetheless a threat to the *Peanuts* patch. They are a threat because they are so easy to get "lost" in—just as were the weeds in Jesus' "parable of the sower" and "parable of the weeds of the field" (Matt. 13). Linus, for example, tries to assure himself that he really does not mind playing right field in the weeds. "The only thing that bothers me is I don't know if I'm *facing* the right way!" he says. In this regard, Snoopy has a very peculiar malady Charlie Brown calls "weed-claustrophobia." This fear enables Snoopy to do a strange thing almost like the Apostle Peter's ability to walk on the water as long as he kept his eyes on his master, and did not look down into the dark waves of the storm (Matt. 14:25-31). For whether Snoopy represents a kind of cosmic catcher in the rye, or comic outfielder in the weeds, he is literally terrified of weeds:

"What's the difference between 'claustrophobia' and '*weed*-claustrophobia'?" Lucy asks Charlie Brown after seeing Snoopy's horror of the weeds. "Regular claustrophobia is *nothing* compared to '*weed*-claustrophobia,'" he explains. Even the very worst sufferings "the natural man" can endure are like a "jest," Kierkegaard tells us, when compared to the dreadful "sickness unto death."[13] "Thus may we gather honey from the weed,/And make a moral of the Devil himself,"[14] as Shakespeare put it; thus Schulz would not seem to be above the same strategem.

But this is the man to whom I will look, he that is humble and contrite in spirit, and trembles at my word.

—Isaiah 66:2

Blessed are the poor in spirit, for theirs is the kingdom of heaven. Blessed are those who mourn, for they shall be comforted.

—Matthew 5:3-4

And have you forgotten the exhortation which addresses you as sons?—"My son, do not regard lightly the discipline of the Lord, nor lose courage when you are punished by him. For the Lord disciplines him whom he loves, and chastises every son whom he receives." It is for discipline that you have to endure. God is treating you as sons; for what son is there whom his father does not discipline? If you are left without discipline, in which all have participated, then you are illegitimate children and not sons . . . . For the moment all discipline seems painful rather than pleasant; later it yields the peaceful fruit of righteousness to those who have been trained by it.

—Hebrews 12:5-8, 11

But adversity is what makes you mature. The growing soul is watered best by tears of sadness.

—Charlie Brown

IV. Good Grief!

"Good grief" may seem to be a contradiction in terms. But actually there are two distinct types of grief—good and not-so-good grief: "For godly grief produces a repentance that leads to salvation and brings no regret, but worldly grief produces death" (2 Cor. 7:10). Consequently Christians can call the day on which Christ was crucified "*Good* Friday." For just as the cross was the shadow through which Christ had to pass in order to overcome death, suffering is also the necessary path for any man who wishes "to walk in newness of life." "The way of Christ" is "the way of the cross"— his cross *and* our own:

We know that our old self was crucified with him so that the sinful body might be destroyed, and we might no longer be enslaved to sin. For he who has died is freed from sin. But if we have died with Christ, we believe that we shall also live with him (Rom. 6:6-8).

The "old self," then, *must* be crucified. If we "must be born anew," the old self first must die. If we are to become "slaves of Jesus

Christ" (Rom. 1:1), we first must be "torn apart" from all the old gods we have originally clung to. Mr. Schulz seems to be pointing to this experience in his own life by saying:

> I grew up an only child, and my mother died the very week I was drafted. This was a tremendous blow to our little family. I was assigned to the 20th Armored Division and eventually became a machine gun squad leader.... we took part in the liberation of Dachau and Munich.... Before going into the Armed Forces I met a minister of the Church of God ... He walked into my father's barbershop one day in St. Paul, Minnesota ... It was not long after that that we called upon him to preach my mother's funeral sermon. After coming back from the Army, I began to attend services at his little church. We had an active group of young people—all of us were in our twenties—and we began studying the Bible together. The more I thought about the matter during those study times, the more I realized that I really loved God. I recognized the fact that he had pulled me through a depression in which I had been torn apart from everything I knew, and that he had enabled me to survive so many experiences.[1]

In a sense, it is a "hard saying" or *bad* news to say that everyone *must* go "through a depression" in order to emerge in a new and infinitely more satisfying life. This is why the gospel, or "good news," is never *good* news except to those who are already "meek and lowly," or "of a humble and contrite spirit"; this is why the gospel is always addressed to those "who have ears to hear"—those "who labor and are heavy laden": "Come to me, all who labor and are heavy laden, and I will give you rest" (Matt. 11:28). But to say that life *must* have its "downs," especially such a *complete* "down" as a prerequisite for reaching a complete "up," is a genuine offense to those who have never been—nor wish to be—*that* discouraged. The problem Lucy is raising below is the so-called "problem of evil," the problem of vindicating the justice of a sovereign God in permitting the existence of suffering. Why must we endure discipline in order to learn? Why must we pass through such a hell of a world in order to get to heaven? Why must there be "downs" along with the "ups"? These are serious questions that have caused many people—from Job to Camus—to rebel violently against the nature of reality. Lucy, who is noted for wanting to go "through life with the

least possible effort on her part," in "sort of a spiritual jet-stream," again kicks against the pricks of reality by shouting, "By the time I'm eighteen, I expect this world to be perfect! Why should I have to live in a world somebody else has messed up?! *I'll give them twelve years to get everything in order!*" "What if they need more time?" asks Charlie Brown. "Tell them not to bother wiring for an extension! The answer will be, '*No!*'" On this side of paradise, the Church has no final answer to "the problem of evil." Paul addressed himself to this problem when he said:

> You will say to me then, "Why does he still find fault? For who can resist his will?" But who are you, a man, to answer back to God? Will what is molded say to its molder, "Why have you made me thus?" (Rom. 9:19-20).

"Where were you when I laid the foundation of the earth? . . . Who determined its measurements—surely you know!" asks the Lord rather sarcastically of Job (Job 38:4-5), thus giving Paul a good precedent to follow. But Paul may have been trying to soften these rather blunt "it-is-none-of-your-business" answers when he said, "I consider that the sufferings of this present time are not worth comparing with the glory that is to be revealed to us" (Rom. 8:18). Nevertheless, the sufferings and evil of the present time are with us, and Christians should never attempt to "explain" them by pretending they do not exist or by not taking them seriously. But finally the Church must point to the mystery of God and say with Paul that as deep as human misery *is,* it is indeed not to be compared to the final triumph of the love of God—"who desires all men to be saved and to come to the knowledge of the truth" (1 Tim. 2:4)—a love made manifest in Jesus Christ, who could say even on the cross, "Father, forgive them; for they know not what they do" (Luke 23:34).

But the Christian is not only a person who is persuaded that God's mercy and love will *finally* triumph for all men. As a man who now enjoys the "first fruits of the Spirit" (Rom. 8:23), he personally can even now "glory in tribulations also" (Rom. 5:3, K.J.V.). For the Christian has learned to drink from the cup of the hard fact—even as Job did—that God "delivers the afflicted by their affliction, and opens their ear by adversity" (Job 36:15). This rather severe means of instruction is necessary because men originally take their lives "for granted," as something *given.* Therefore, unless everything men know is at some time *radically* threatened, and is only then *for-given* to them, can they ever really appreciate the gift of life to its fullest. Thus the pattern of God's pedagogy resembles the following scene, in which Snoopy wakes up on top of his doghouse to learn the answer to the question: "What does it have to snow for?!"

"Behold, God does all these things, twice, three times, with a man, to bring back his soul from the Pit, that he may see the light of life" (Job 33:29-30). But this lesson did not come easily to Job either, just as Snoopy's "awakening" was a rather rude one. ("Life is full of rude awakenings," Snoopy once observed.) In the midst of Job's terrible sufferings he cried out to God: "Thou hast turned cruel to me; with the might of thy hand thou dost persecute me" (Job 30:21). But finally, after whole chapters of "defending his ways" and even revolting, Job is brought around to the position that indeed "the fear of the Lord, that is wisdom" (Job 28:28). This kind of divine instruction in "Christmas programs" may be brought about through a *holy* terror:

And all the world *is* taxed—but especially Linus. Therefore Linus would probably not only appreciate Job's ordeal, but also have great sympathy for the psalmist who wrote: "Before I was afflicted I went astray; but now I keep thy word" (Ps. 119:67). For "it is a fearful thing to fall into the hands of the living God" (Heb. 10:31). But it is through this infinitely more dreadful fear of *God* that Christians are persuaded to keep God's word not only for themselves, but "knowing the fear of the Lord, we persuade men" (2 Cor. 5:11). Hence the same requirement given to St. Paul is given to all Christians: "For necessity is laid upon me. Woe to me if I do not preach the gospel!" (1 Cor. 9:16). Only until one accepts the necessity imposed by this greater woe, will the mere fears of our parts in a universal "Christmas program" cease being hard on the nervous system. For the fear of the *Lord* (that is, Lucy's fist), makes all other fears look insignificant indeed. As Kierkegaard put it, "Such is the way a man always acquires courage; when one fears a greater danger, it is as though the other did not exist."[2]

The Church is the world's great lost and found department. It assumes that all men are originally lost, are moving relentlessly in the wrong direction, but that they do not know it; it also assumes that what they do not consciously know not only will—but *does*—hurt them. Therefore the Church also believes that before men can be found, they must first come to a personally *deep* awareness of being deeply lost. For only in this way can they then reverse directions, find an infinitely more satisfying way, and thus come to a personally *elated* appreciation of having found this way—or having been found by it. This is why Christ could say, "he who is forgiven little, loves little" (Luke 7:47). This also is why in the New Testament there is more rejoicing over finding one *lost* sheep "than over the ninety-nine ·that never went astray" (Matt. 18:13); or there is more rejoicing over the return of the *prodigal* son, who had "come to himself" by realizing how lost he was, than there was for the son who never left home in the first place (Luke 15:11-32). And just as a person must become lost before he can be found, he must also seek before he can find. For if that which is most valuable to us—our very life, for instance—is lost, *hopelessly* and *impossibly* lost, and *then* is somehow found, we will appreciate even more gratefully its having been found. If it turns out that the lost is practically found for us, right under our noses, we may be a little humbled:

 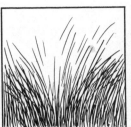 

We know well that the seeker does not always have to wander far afield, since the more sacred the object of his search the nearer it is to him; and if he seeks Thee, O God, Thou art of all things most near! But we know also that that seeking is never without its pains and its temptation, how then would there not be fear in seeking Thee, who art mighty![3]

Thus the transition from lost to found is never an easy one. It is never easy to be a prodigal son—or daughter. It is never easy to say, "I will arise and go to my father, and will say to him, 'Father, I have sinned against heaven and before you; I am no longer worthy to be called your son; treat me as one of your hired servants'" (Luke 15:18, 19). This is never easy, because it is not until our situation becomes *completely hopeless* that we can humble ourselves to the extent of admitting that such a gross mistake was our own. As St. Paul put it, "I would rather die than have any one deprive me of my ground for boasting" (1 Cor. 9:15). And in a sense this is of course what *must* happen—one must die. Therefore repentance—or "returning"—is never easy. But it is only when we *do* repent that our father gives us what amounts to the "birthday party" that he has long wanted to give us: "Bring the fatted calf and kill it, and let us eat and make merry; for this my son was dead, and is alive again; he was lost, and is found" (Luke 15:23-24):

Grief, then, always has a *paradoxical* relationship to the Christian: it is "grief," but it is "good." The fear of the Lord is the beginning of that wisdom that casts out all fear; therefore this holy fear is also seen by the Christian as being a great gift. Life has the least chance of "passing us by" as long as it is always "knocking us down and walking all over us," to use Charlie Brown's salty language. Or, to use the language of Christ, "whoever would save his life will lose it; and whoever loses his life for my sake and the gospel's will save it" (Mark 8:35). "When I am weak, then I am strong" (2 Cor. 12: 10), says Paul on one side of this paradox; "I'm never quite so stupid as when I'm being smart," admits Linus on the other. For

"God chose what is foolish in the world to shame the wise, God chose what is weak in the world to shame the strong, God chose what is low and despised in the world, even things that are not, to bring to nothing things that are, so that no human being might boast in the presence of God" (1 Cor. 1:27-29). "Therefore," says Luther, "when God makes alive, He kills; when He justifies, He imposes guilt; when He leads us to heaven, He thrusts us down into hell."[4]

The paradoxical quality of God's love—which afflicts the comfortable and comforts the afflicted—often seems to be illustrated in *Peanuts* by the use of two distinct symbols. First, there is the *rain;* for the Li'l Folks are cheered and checked by the selfsame sky.

God's love always appears as judgment, or wrath, whenever we attempt to judge him. Thus God frustrated the devices of the crafty builders of the Old Testament's "Tower of Babel," who wished to "ascend into heaven . . . that is, to bring Christ down" (Rom. 10:6), as St. Paul would put it. "We must not put the Lord to the test," warns Paul, unless we ourselves wish to be tested severely by the Lord, "the Destroyer" (1 Cor. 10:9-12). This also means man cannot "prove" God's existence any more than God can. Such attempts would require an infallible "third party" to act as the judge of God, when God himself must be the only ultimate judge if he is to be God. "God can no more prove his existence . . . than he can swear; he has nothing higher to swear by," said Kierkegaard.[5] If we require some kind of sign, or "proof," for our belief in God, then we believe, or place our trust, not in God but in the sign or proof. "An evil and adulterous generation seeks for a sign," said Christ to the Pharisees, who "to test him . . . asked him to show them a sign from heaven" (Matt. 16:4, 1). Properly, the only "proof" for God's existence—indeed the only proof for "all things" (John 14:26) known by the Christian—is God's own disclosure of himself and his will to the heart of the individual believer. For "it is the Spirit himself bearing witness with our spirit that we are children of God" (Rom. 8:16). But men will insist on having their "signs," whether these signs appear as miracles, scientific demonstrations, rational arguments, or any other objective "third term"; therefore men will also have their judgment from God, whether this judgment appears as rain, frustration, or—as it appeared in "The Tower of Babel" incident (Gen. 11:1-9)—"confusion of their language."

In relation to this subject, one of the towering scientific experiments of the present age appeared in *Peanuts* strips of three successive Sundays. In the first strip, Charlie Brown disgustedly walks off the baseball diamond saying, "Rats! Every time you want to do something it rains!" But Linus, true to Lucy's contention that he does not "know enough to come in out of the rain," remains standing on the playing field. He then lifts up his head and addresses the heavens: "Rain, rain, go away. Come again some other day!" Suddenly it stops raining; whereupon Linus, scared out of his wits, runs home as fast as he can, slams the door behind him, and begs of Lucy, "Hide me!" On the following Sunday, Linus is standing in the rain with Lucy, explaining to her what had happened. Again he repeats the magic incantation; again it immediately stops raining. "Frightening, isn't it?" he asks her. "I didn't know whether I should call a doctor or a booking agent. Do you think I'm a demon? Do you think maybe they'll stone me? *I don't wanna be stoned!!*" But Lucy calms him down by saying, "Take it easy. We don't know for sure yet that it was your doing. It's only happened twice. If you can do it *once* more, then we'll know for sure. We'll just have to wait for it to start raining again." (Pause) "I wonder if I can be patented?" asks Linus. The next Sunday is the day of the "big scientific moment":

"And Jesus answered him, 'It is said, "You shall not tempt the Lord your God" ' " (Luke 4:12). For as H. Richard Niebuhr put it, the God of the Bible "is not the object of magic practices whereby his power may be gained for the pursuit of human ends, as is the case in many religions."[6] The implications of this point of view for much of what passes as "prayer" should be obvious.

But just as God "sends rain on the just and on the unjust" (Matt. 5:45), the love God bestows on all men can be felt either as a blessing or as a judgment, depending on one's faith or lack of faith. Charlie Brown, for instance, who on one occasion sorrowfully declared, "It always rains on the unloved!" was once "saved by the rain!" when one of his inevitably lost baseball games was rained out. In the following cartoon Snoopy is blessed even as he is "dying of thirst," for he is "satisfied" by the rain. But also in this cartoon, Schulz seems to be using the rain to say, in another way, what we have seen him suggest before: God's "free gift" of grace through Jesus Christ cannot be limited to any man-made channel for that grace. "I don't even like the expression, 'take communion,' " Schulz has said. "You cannot 'take' communion. You are a part of the communion. You are communing with Christ; you are a part of the community of saints."[7] Therefore, "let him who is thirsty come, let him who desires take the water of life without price" (Rev. 22:17):

THAT'S ONE I'M GOING TO HAVE TO THINK ABOUT FOR AWHILE!

Schulz gives all of us a lot of high-protein food for thought; but just as Snoopy indicates in the above cartoon, the job of unshelling *Peanuts* is largely up to us.

The second notable symbol in *Peanuts* that seems to represent the paradoxical nature of God's love, is the *tree*. Even more than rain, the tree has been used as this kind of symbol in the Bible and in art. For the tree is a traditional Christian symbol for the cross—itself the central symbol of Christianity, representing suffering and death as well as peace and life. Through Christ, Christians obtain "peace by the blood of his cross" (Col. 1:20); and yet the cross is "the stumbling block" which cannot be "removed" (Gal. 5:11) from the only path leading to the highest life available to man. The cross, or tree, is that point at which one must either risk everything, or settle for far less than one had hoped. When the rich young man came to Christ and asked him, "what must I do to inherit eternal life?" Christ told him, "One thing thou lackest: go thy way, sell whatsoever thou hast, and give to the poor, and thou shalt have treasure in heaven: and come, take up the cross, and follow me. And he was

sad at that saying, and went away grieved: for he had great pos-
sessions" (Mark 10:21-22, K.J.V.):

"The Preacher" of Ecclesiastes tells us over and over that all of
man's hopes, dreams, and efforts—apart from his "fear of God"—
are, as he puts it, "vanity and a striving after wind" (Eccles. 2:11).
Certainly all of Charlie Brown's hope, dreams, and efforts seems to
be vanity and a quite literal "striving after wind," for they seem to
be summed up in his kites, which he is never able to get quite off the
ground. Why? Because they usually meet with the barrier of the
tree, every kind of tree imaginable: a tiny miniature tree placed
outside Violet's dollhouse, the Christmas tree Schroeder is trying to

bring home, the innocent little sapling that Linus and Lucy have just planted, etc. In a desperate effort to fly a *single* kite, Charlie Brown once tried flying four kites at one time, but each became hung on a separate tree. Like Melville's Ahab, helplessly bound to the white whale Moby Dick by his own entangled harpoon line, Charlie Brown has also been bound to his invincible foe, the tree, by his own hopelessly snarled kite string. Thus Charlie Brown surely would share St. Paul's appreciation for a certain Old Testament statement; as Paul phrased it, "Cursed be every one who hangs on a tree" (Gal. 3:13; Deut. 21:23):

And there does seem to be some kind of curse on Charlie Brown, for the tree always appears in one form or another for him to get hung on. It is a shame perhaps that it seems *always* to have to be this way, but evidently Christ was quite emphatic when he said, "If any man would come after me, let him deny himself and take up his cross and follow me" (Matt. 16:24; Mark 8:34; Luke 9:23):

Indeed, as Patty once pointed out to Violet, "With Charlie Brown, flying a kite is an emotional experience."

But it is important to note that for Charlie Brown, just as for the Christian, the tree, or cross, which is first met as his archenemy and final stumbling-block, has the amazing ability of becoming his central support and refuge—especially in times of great trouble:

Such is the way one always learns the meaning of "good grief."
Only "when life gets too hard" does one discover that trees "are very
good to lean against." For "as a father pities his children, so the
LORD pities those who fear him" (Ps. 103:13).

God needs MEN, not creatures
Full of noisy, catchy phrases.
Dogs he asks for, who their noses
Deeply thrust into—To-day,
And there scent Eternity.[1]

And behold, a Canaanite woman . . . came out and cried, "Have
mercy on me, O Lord, Son of David . . . ." He answered, "I was
sent only to the lost sheep of the house of Israel." But she came
and knelt before him, saying, "Lord, help me." And he answered,
"It is not fair to take the children's bread and throw it to the
dogs." She said, "Yes, Lord, yet even the dogs eat the crumbs that
fall from their master's table." Then Jesus answered her, "O
woman, great is your faith! Be it done for you as you desire."
                                                —*Matthew 15:22, 24-28*

Anything that falls on the floor is legally mine.
                                                —*Snoopy*

V. The Hound of Heaven

In the following lines, Shakespeare has expressed beautifully the
Christian's view of the paradoxical role that great suffering plays in
men's lives:

But whate'er I be,
Nor I, nor any man that but man is,
With nothing shall be pleased till he be eased
With being nothing.[2]

In other words, "God creates everything out of nothing," as Kierkegaard put it, "and everything which God is to use he first reduces
to nothing."[3]

Charlie Brown is quite familiar—but is never eased—"with being
nothing." "You know why that little red-haired girl never notices
me?" Charlie, almost in tears, asks Linus. "Because I'm nothing!
When she looks over here, there's nothing to see! How can she see
someone who's nothing?!" (Pause) "You're depressed, aren't you?"
asks Linus, using his best client-centered approach. But Charlie is
still not eased. For him, it is simply not enough to say that "life has
its ups and downs," or that "grief is finally good," or that "we learn
more from losing than we do from winning":

How is one eased with being nothing? *What* is found in the midst of grief that makes even grief become good? *What* can transform even losing into winning? Decidedly, Christianity knows nothing among men "except Jesus Christ and him crucified" (1 Cor. 2:2). Consequently, whenever Christianity fails to hold these two essential factors in unity—so that it tends to proclaim either a Christ without a cross or a cross without a Christ—it becomes something other than Christianity, although it may still limp along under the banner of "Christianity." Thus far we have been emphasizing the *cross*, or the *grief*, or the "nothingness," or the "aaaughh!" essential to the Christian life. But now we turn to that factor that *enables* our grief to become good, that produces the light that shines in the darkness, that brings ease even into the midst of dis-ease, that transforms the cross from a symbol of death to a symbol of new life and hope— we now turn more directly to the element of redemption expressed in

Peanuts by extremely subtle suggestion, we now turn to Jesus Christ.

Snoopy we would hesitate to call "Christ." He comes closer, rather, to being "a little Christ"—that is, a Christian. For as Schulz himself has pointed out, Snoopy is capable of being "one of the meanest" members of the entire *Peanuts* cast.[4] Furthermore, Snoopy has other faults (or "character traits," as Linus likes to refer to "faults"): he is lazy, he is a "chow hound" without parallel, he is bitingly sarcastic, he is frequently a coward, and he often becomes quite weary of being what he is basically—a dog. He is, in other words, a fairly drawn caricature for what is probably the typical Christian. And if anyone should have any illusions about how "good" all Christians are, he would only need to read one of Paul's letters to "the Saints" in Rome or Corinth to realize that "Saints" often have a few readjustments to make before they become complete angels. Also, it is good to remember Luther's teaching here that "Ecclesia est abscondita," the Church is hidden, for it lives by faith and not by sight or works. "He who would look at an act as such sees no difference between a Christian and a non-Christian," Luther reminds us.[5] Then how is one to distinguish between the Christian and the non-Christian? Finally, this is a judgment only God can make; but there are certain guideposts available for intelligent guesses. For instance, "By this all men will know that you are my disciples, if you have love for one another" (John 13:35). And in spite of his many rather questionable "character traits," by this test Snoopy does rather well:

The dog, because of his "wonderful qualities of love, loyalty, watch-fulness and courage" (Charlie Brown's description), often has been used as a symbol for *faith* in literature and art; it is even used in this way in the Bible. But the dog also is a good symbol for faith as there is a real sense in which a man must become "as a dog" before he can become a Christian. He must take on the dog's lowliness of complete obedience and humility at the feet of his master and in service to others. He must be willing, as a dog, and as was the Canaanite woman who fell to her knees before Jesus, to "eat the crumbs that fall from the master's table," before the master will say, ". . . great is your faith! Be it done for you as you desire." When the great German philosopher Hegel scoffed at Schleiermacher's declaration that at the core of religious faith was .the feeling of *absolute de-pendence,* Hegel said that of all creatures, then, the most religious must be the dog. In this, Hegel was closer to the truth than he realized.

Snoopy, as a little Christ, quite obviously takes on Christ's am-bivalent work of humbling the exalted and exalting the humble, "that those who do not see may see, and that those who see may become blind" (John 9:39), as Jesus put it. "The love that follows us sometimes is our trouble,/Which still we thank as love,"[6] quoth Shakespeare. And Snoopy is certainly a troubling love that follows. For as his name implies, Snoopy is given to constant prying and meddling. None of the popular false gods of the *Peanuts* patch are secure when he is around. He is a "hound of heaven," fled from "down the labyrinthine ways," who uses his snoopy nose to smell out faults not immediately discernible to the eye. "The eye can be deceived, but the nose knows!" he tells us. As an illustration of Snoopy's hounding after strange gods, first consider the following:

> But as to the times and the seasons, brethren . . . you yourselves know well that the day of the Lord will come like a thief in the night. When people say, "There is peace and security," then sudden destruction will come upon them as travail comes upon a woman with child, and there will be no escape (1 Thess. 5:1-3).

Now notice how in the nutshell of the following single cartoon, Schulz manages to incorporate every essential element of the above quotation. Snoopy has stealthily crept up on Linus. And then—

On the other hand, it is Snoopy who saves his friends from the doom of too much—or the wrong kind of—security, when this backfires on them or when they finally do fall:

Snoopy, like the Lord, "wounds, but he binds up; he smites, but his hands heal" (Job 5:18). His discriminating attitude ("For my kind, the story of civilization has always left much to be desired!") often wounds his more "civilized" friends. But he binds up: On one occasion Lucy decided she would break Linus' "stupid blanket habit" once and for all. The difficulty in this attempt was that it came closer to breaking Linus than it did the habit.

After two weeks of Linus' pitiful agony and futile digging for his blanket ("Now I know what they mean when they say our future lies in the soil!" he tells Charlie Brown), it is easy to guess who finally saved him from what looked like an imminent "nervous breakdown." Lucy's mistake was that she did not take Eliot's advice in "The Wasteland"—in an obvious reference to Christ—to "keep the Dog far hence, that's friend to men/Or with his nails he'll dig it up again!"[7]

But generally Snoopy, like Lucy, also is trying to get Linus' blanket away from him. "I think I'll use the ol' surprise attack, the way my wolf ancestors did," he once said; whereupon he has the blanket rudely jerked out of his mouth to find that Linus has nailed one end of the blanket to the floor. And so it is that all men yearn to have "the truth," or their security, "nailed down," as the expression goes. The irony in this desire is that this is precisely what God has done for all men—he has had "the truth" (John 14:6) *nailed down.*

As the "Dominican" of *Peanuts*—the *Domini canis,* or "dog of God"—Snoopy is subject to frequent *humiliations,* not the least of which are similar to those of the "suffering servant" of Isaiah: ". . . his appearance was so marred, beyond human semblance, and his form beyond that of the sons of men. . . . He was despised and rejected by men . . . and acquainted with grief" (Isa. 52:14; 53:3).

Notice how the following cartoon parallels the following passage of
Scripture, in which Christ is attempting to wash the feet of his
disciples:

> Peter said to him, "You shall never wash my feet." Jesus an-
> swered him, "If I do not wash you, you have no part in me."
> Simon Peter said to him, "Lord, not my feet only but also my
> hands and head!" (John 13:8-9).

But perhaps the most unkindest cut of all for Snoopy was that classic
advent experience in *Peanuts* in which "the expected one" appeared, but was not actually the one expected. For Snoopy, like
Christ, must know how it feels to show up on an obscure little plot of

ground, and only as a rather disappointing token for the one actually
hoped for:

Nevertheless, Snoopy has learned to live in the doghouse and be con-
tent there. Perhaps this is why he is so fond of Van Gogh. (He
keeps a cherished Van Gogh in his doghouse.) For Van Gogh also
became reconciled to being "a dog." In words that could very well
be applied to Snoopy, Van Gogh wrote of himself:

> ... but the beast has a human history, and though only a dog, he
> has a human soul, and even a very sensitive one, that makes him
> feel what people think of him, which an ordinary dog cannot
> do ... I consciously choose *the dog's path through life;* I will

remain a *dog,* I shall be *poor. . .* I want to *remain human*—going *into* nature.[8]

Likewise, the weed-fearing Snoopy is no ordinary dog. For he is not only sensitive to what people think of him; he also exhibits a peculiar concern for others—and even for other "things" of nature, such as the *leaves* that fall from the trees. "I'm going to have to stop watching those leaves fall," he once said. "I get so depressed I can't sleep nights!" But perhaps this depression is not so difficult to understand. "Withered" and "falling leaves" are used frequently in the Bible as images for those in whom the wellsprings of faith have dried up, for those who "in time of temptation fall away." In this sense, then, to fall from the tree is truly "to die":

"You don't know it," says Snoopy to one fallen leaf, "but your troubles are just beginning!" For "I am the vine, you are the

branches," said Christ. "If a man does not abide in me, he is cast
forth as a branch and withers; and the branches are gathered,
thrown into the fire and burned" (John 15:6). But Snoopy also
believes in "the forgiveness of sins." He is not like the narrow
legalists who neglect "the weightier matters of the law, justice and
mercy and faith" (Matt. 23:23). Indeed, as a theologian, his in-
sights are usually far more astute than those of whom he follows:

Although Snoopy is certainly familiar with the humiliations that
come with being a dog, he also seems to know the *joy* inherent in
these humiliations: "Blessed are you when men hate you, and when
they exclude you and revile you, and cast out your name as evil, on
account of the Son of man! Rejoice in that day, and leap for joy,
for behold, your reward is great in heaven" (Luke 6:22). Snoopy is
constantly "leaping for joy." Not even the no-nonsense Lucy can

discourage his joyful dancing. "Happiness isn't everything, you know!" she shouts at the happily bounding Snoopy. "It'll never bring you peace of mind!" she continues, as he peacefully dances on by her. It also may be that Snoopy has been reading Havelock Ellis. (It is known that Snoopy reads a great deal; although we are "disillusioned," as Lucy is, to learn "he moves his lips when he reads!") Dancing is "the supreme symbol of spiritual life," says Ellis. "For dancing is the loftiest, the most moving, the most beautiful of the arts, because it is no mere translation or abstraction from life; it is life itself."9 "To those of us with real understanding," agrees Snoopy, "dancing is the only pure art form."

This is the kind of "living" Paul was talking about when he said, "He who through faith is righteous shall live" (Rom. 1:17). For in faith there is a "living" or a "joy no man taketh from you" (John 16:22, K.J.V.).

> For I am sure that neither death, nor life, nor angels, nor principalities, nor things present, nor things to come, nor powers, nor height, nor depth, nor anything else in all creation, will be able to separate us from the love of God in Christ Jesus our Lord (Rom. 8:38-39).

Finally, Lucy and Snoopy happily dance off together. "If you can't lick 'em, join 'em!" she explains cheerfully.

Snoopy also is a good symbol for faith as his total outward distinctiveness can be representative of the infinite inward difference between the Christian and the non-Christian. For "if any man is in Christ," said Paul, "he is a new creature" (2 Cor. 5:17). Furthermore, Snoopy's minority exclusiveness can serve to illustrate that "a Christian is a rare bird," as Luther put it. For God not only "chose what is low and despised in the world" (1 Cor. 1:28), but also—as Christ said—"few are chosen" (Matt. 22:14). Snoopy seems to realize that his lowliness and lonely separation mean beatitude, that he is "rejected by men but in God's sight chosen and precious" (1 Pet. 2:4). For to be a Christian is to be "a little Christ"; and to be "the Christ" is to be the anointed one, the chosen one, the one who is specially called-out, set apart, or elected— it is to be "the lucky one."

Snoopy's being "the lucky one" may also help to explain why the happiness of the Li'l Folks seems dependent to an extent on their relationship to him. "Happiness is a warm puppy!" says Lucy in one strip, as she pats Snoopy on the head and gives him a big hug. But on another occasion: "You know what I've noticed about you, Lucy?" Charlie Brown asks as they walk past Snoopy. "I've noticed that you never pat a dog on the head when you walk by him." "So what?" asks Lucy. "So it proves you're just not an animal lover, that's all." "Worse than that," Snoopy reflects, "it's a symptom of a deeper illness!" A deeper illness indeed! For "truly, I say to you," instructed Christ, "as you did it not to one of the least of these, you did it not to me" (Matt. 25:45).

Schulz has said that "If you are a Christian . . . you are one of the 'called-out ones,' who have been called out to serve God."[10] The "called of Jesus Christ," or "God's elect," is a central category in the New Testament. For to "the called" has been given the happy "mystery hidden for ages and generations but now made manifest to his saints" (Col. 1:26); to those lucky enough to be *called* of God, "has been given the secret of the kingdom of God, but for those outside everything is in parables" (Mark 4:11):

Just as God "was in the world ... yet the world knew him not" (John 1:10), the Christian also is often incognito; for likewise the Christian's strength usually appears only as weakness. This is because the Christian, like Christ, in order to save men not only dwells among the least of men, but also dwells among them as the very least of the least, indeed as their *servant*. Therefore, the Christian, like Christ, usually appears to the world as only a kind of little man's watchdog (who "always gets the leftovers"), just as Snoopy keeps watch at night from the top of his doghouse over the sleeping Charlie Brown. But Snoopy must know that, in spite of his status "out back," "the glory of the LORD shall be your rear guard" (Isa. 58:8). Hence he can say, "I dwell in the high and holy place, and also with him who is of a contrite and humble spirit, to revive the spirit of the humble, and to revive the heart of the contrite" (Isa. 57:15). Thus it is probably Snoopy's resemblance to these strange people called "Christians"—"a peculiar people, zealous of good works" (Titus 2:14, K.J.V.)—that makes it seem wise to be on guard even against this most harmless of all guardians:

See you now,
Your bait of falsehood takes this carp of truth.
And thus do we of wisdom and of reach . . .
By indirections find directions out.

—*Hamlet, II, i*

I cannot fail to be thrilled every time I read the things that Jesus
said, and I am more and more convinced of the necessity of following him. What Jesus means to me is this: In him we are able to
see God, and to understand his feelings toward us.

—*Schulz*[1]

If one of two persons, who are telling silly stories, uses language
with a double meaning, understood in his own circle, while the
other uses it with only one meaning, any one not in the secret,
who hears them both talk in this manner, will pass upon them
the same judgment. But if afterwards, in the rest of their conversation one says angelic things, and the other always dull com-
monplaces, he will judge that the one spoke in mysteries, and not
the other; the one having sufficiently shown that he is incapable
of such foolishness, and capable of being mysterious; and the other
that he is incapable of mystery, and capable of foolishness.

—*Pascal*[2]

VI. Concluding Unscientific Postscript

By this point, it may have struck the reader as a bit incongruous
to couple such a "serious matter," the Christian message, with the
comic, or the humorous. Therefore we should perhaps point out that
in addition to the Christian faith's relevance to all areas of life,
Christianity also has a *special* relation to the comic. "Christianity . . .
is the most humorous point of view in the history of the world."[3]

There are several reasons why "what we preach" turns out to be
comic or "folly" or "the foolishness of God," to use Paul's terms.
The first involves the very nature of love, or belief, itself. In the
history of western literature there is probably a no more popular
subject for comedy than the complete blindness of love, of the lover
who insists on making a fool of himself simply because his passions
have the upper hand over his reason. Both love and faith can

never give a *reason* for their love; they can only say, "This is my beloved" (Song of Sol. 5:16). But perhaps this is just as well; for if the lover, or believer, could give us a "reason" for loving his love, such as her great "beauty" or "charm" or "wealth," then it is quite obvious that the lover would not actually be in love with his "love," but that his *real* heart's desire would be beauty or charm or wealth or *whatever* his "reason" might be for loving the supposed object of his love. Thus it is impossible for one to have this kind of ulterior motive and remain a *true* lover, whether on the divine *or* human level; this is why the Christian faith finally is "dogmatic" on one side of the coin, "confessional" on the other. "Jesus Christ is the Son of God because he is so,"[4] says dogmatics; or, if you *must* have a reason, "Jesus Christ is the Son of God because he has spoken *directly* to my heart that he is so," says Christian confession. This blind faith, or love, always gives the Christian a certain comic aspect:

But if the *nature* of belief is a good subject for comedy, *what* the Christian believes can be considered even more comic—for basically the Christian faith is absurd, impossible, and foolish; it is "a stumbling block to the Jews and folly to the Gentiles" (1 Cor. 1:23); it is not only *without* reason, but it is positively an *offense* to man's reason. Basic Christian tenets such as "maker of heaven and earth," the Incarnation, the Holy Spirit, "the resurrection of the body," and "the life everlasting" are simply impossible nonsense when judged on the basis of what natural man knows about himself and his world. Why, one would have to become like a *child* to believe these things! But, again, this is precisely why Christ said, "Whoever humbles himself like this child, he is the greatest in the kingdom of heaven" (Matt. 18:4):

Thus "all things are possible to him who believes" (Mark 9:23), even if this belief usually makes the believer himself look impossible.

There is another, even more basic, reason for the Christian faith's close kinship with comedy: Christianity, like comedy, always involves a *genuine* fall, or reversal, that is nevertheless not *ultimately* serious. This is why the story of the creation, fall, and subsequent redemption of all men is finally a "divine comedy." When Charlie Brown's kite falls smashing to the ground, and he screams, "I'll *never* be able to get that kite in the air! *Never, never, never, never!*" we are inclined to laugh when we then see Snoopy flying the same kite from the top of his doghouse, while lying comfortably on his back. But when King Lear falls down on stage with his murdered daughter in his arms, both to rise again "Never, never, never, never, never," and then the final curtain falls, we find this scene difficult to regard as humorous. Indeed, some aestheticians have contended that such a thing as "Christian tragedy" is a contradiction in terms. Paradoxically, however, when the Christian begins to take in *utter* seriousness the "appalling strangeness of the mercy of God,"[5] he then learns not to take too seriously the worldly situation of any *man*. Graham Greene has expressed this hope forcefully in *The Heart of the Matter* in his use of the following lines by Rilke:

> We are all falling. This hand's falling too—all have this falling sickness none withstands. And yet there's always One whose gentle hands this universal falling can't fall through.[6]

Just as in all comedy there is a final redemption, Christianity contends there is a final redemption for all: "For as in Adam all die, so also in Christ shall all be made alive" (1 Cor. 15:22). Therefore the laughter of comedy and the joy of Christ's gospel are *closely* related.

Schulz has said:

> I am a great believer in what the church calls "holy living." I think life should be lived on as pure a scale as possible.... I am not suggesting that we take ourselves out of the world, of course;

we still have our obligations, and we must live in the area where God has placed us, exerting our influence and working with schools and institutions. We have to do the best we can, living each day at the point where it begins, but this does not mean that life cannot be lived in a holy way.[7]

Does this mean then that every man can be a minister for Christ regardless of where he is or what work he is involved in? Does this mean that it is possible—nay, imperative!—that every Christian learn how to express his faith not only in his words, but also in his entire life and work? Does this even mean that a Christian might find himself placed by God in the improbable position of a *cartoonist,* and still find ways and means of "exerting his influence" (for those who have eyes to see) in and through cartoons? We take it Mr. Schulz's statement does mean all of this; and we further take it that this is precisely what he has been doing in his cartoons. To be sure, Schulz basically is "in the business of trying to draw funny pictures for tomorrow's paper."[8] But Schulz "uses his folly like a stalking-horse, and under the presentation of that, he shoots his wit."[9] We would not have the reader think that every *Peanuts* cartoon contains some profound theological meaning. If this were the case, Schulz probably could not keep his audience with him any more than a Shakespeare could if he had composed his plays of nothing but Hamlet-like soliloquys. But on the other hand, as Schulz has pointed out, "if you do not say anything in a cartoon, you might as well not draw it at all!" The Christian faith must learn to speak meaningfully to men where they are; and when it comes to "serious" reading, there are probably many people who never get far beyond the comics section of the daily newspaper, who read only the comics "religiously." Therefore, in keeping with Paul's formula, we can see how it might be possible for a Christian to say, "To the readers of cartoons, I became a cartoonist." Christians, like Paul, are never concerned with "taking themselves out of the world," but rather necessarily find themselves becoming all things to all men, that they might—*by all means*—save some (Rom. 9:22). Everything the Christian does—*absolutely everything*—is for "edification," for the communication of Christ's gospel; and insofar as it "is not in the last resort edifying [it] is precisely for that reason not Christian."[10]   "Let all things be done for edification" (1 Cor. 14:26), said Paul; for this is precisely what it means "to love one another" *and* to love God. Therefore, "If I speak in the tongues of men and of angels, but have not love, I am a noisy gong or a clanging cymbal" (1 Cor. 13:1) — just as Linus is a "noisy gong" in the following cartoon, in which he plays the role of a miniature "Jonathan Swift in reverse" (Swift once said he loved people, but hated mankind):

Peanuts lends itself easily to this kind of Christian interpretation, whether these thoughts were always in the artist's mind or not. Thus *Peanuts*—and countless other efforts in the modern arts—can play a vital part in the life of the Church by providing meaning-full "conversation pieces" between the Church and culture, by being wonderfully imaginative parables of and for our times, and by giving the Church a creative and effective opportunity for making an even more direct witness for its Lord. For all Christian witness will finally be a *direct* witness—to stand up and be counted or to wear one's heart on one's sleeve unmistakably for Jesus Christ's sake, confessing him alone to be Lord and Savior. Christians should always remember, however, never to be too disappointed if this witness is never really heard or understood by those whom they love; because the "success" of all Christian witnessing finally lies in the hands of God.

But be of good cheer, Charlie Brown! For after all is said and done, there *is* someone who loves you—and this "someone" is only a very humble, peanut-sized representative for One much greater than he:

Amen.

Notes

I. THE CHURCH AND THE ARTS

1. Charles Schulz, "Knowing You Are Not Alone," *Decision,* Vol. IV (Sept., 1963), p. 9.
2. Paul Tillich, *Theology of Culture,* ed. Robert C. Kimball (New York: Oxford University Press, 1959), p. 201.
3. Søren Kierkegaard, *The Point of View for My Work as an Author* (New York: Harper & Brothers, 1962), p. 41.
4. *The Journals of Søren Kierkegaard,* ed. and tr. Alexander Dru (London: Oxford University Press, 1938), p. 232.
5. T. S. Eliot, "Burnt Norton," *The Complete Poems and Plays, 1909-1950* (New York: Harcourt, Brace & World, Inc., 1952), p. 121.
6. Karl Barth, *Dogmatics in Outline,* tr. G. T. Thomson (New York: Philosophical Library, 1949), p. 152.
7. J. D. Salinger, *Franny and Zooey* (Boston: Little, Brown and Company, 1961), p. 164.
8. Karl Barth, *The Epistle to the Romans,* tr. Edwyn C. Hoskyns (London: Oxford University Press, 1933), pp. 115 ff.
9. *Hamlet,* III, ii.
10. Quoted in Søren Kierkegaard, *Stages on Life's Way,* tr. Walter Lowrie (Princeton: Princeton University Press, 1940), p. 26.
11. *Hamlet,* II, ii.
12. "Religion and the Mission of the Artist," in *The New Orpheus,* ed. Nathan A. Scott, Jr. (New York: Sheed and Ward, 1964), p. 63.
13. Schulz, *op. cit.,* p. 9.
14. *Ibid.*
15. Bernhard W. Anderson, *Rediscovering the Bible* (New York: Association Press, 1951), p. 21.
16. Ernst Cassirer, *Mythical Thought,* tr. Ralph Manheim, Vol. II of *Philosophy of Symbolic Forms* (New Haven: Yale University Press, 1955), p. 252.
17. Walter R. Bowie, *Interpreter's Bible* (New York: Abingdon Press, 1951), Vol. VII, p. 165.
18. *Hamlet,* II, ii.
19. Quoted in Barth, *The Epistle to the Romans, op. cit.,* p. 39.
20. Daniel D. Williams, *What Present-Day Theologians Are Thinking,* rev. ed. (New York: Harper & Row, Publishers, 1959), p. 31.
21. *Van Gogh: A Self-Portrait,* ed. W. H. Auden (Greenwich, Conn.: New York Graphic Society, 1961), p. 302.
22. Schulz, *op. cit.,* p. 9.
23. *Ibid.,* pp. 8-9; "A Handful of Peanuts," *Look,* Vol. 22, No. 15 (July 22, 1958), pp. 66-68; "Good Grief; Curly Hair," *Newsweek,* Vol. LVII, No. 10 (March 6, 1961), pp. 68, 71; "The Success of an Utter Failure," *Saturday Evening Post,* Vol. 229, No. 28 (Jan. 12, 1957), pp. 34-35, 70-72; "Good Grief, Charlie Schulz!" *Saturday Evening Post* (April 25, 1964), pp. 26-27; "Child's Garden of Reverses," *Time,* Vol. LXXI, No. 9 (March 3, 1958), p. 58; Stephen Becker, *Comic Art in America* (New York: Simon and Schuster, 1959), pp. 361-366.
24. "Good Grief; Curly Hair," *op. cit.,* p. 68.

25. Søren Kierkegaard, quoted in Barth, *The Epistle to the Romans, op. cit.*, pp. 98-99.
26. Samuel L. Bethell, *Essays on Literary Criticism and the English Tradition* (New York: Hillary House Publishers, Ltd., 1948), p. 25.
27. T. S. Eliot, *The Use of Poetry and the Use of Criticism* (London: Faber and Faber Limited, 1933), p. 31.
28. "Religion and Literature," in *Selected Essays of T. S. Eliot* (New York: Harcourt, Brace and Company, 1950), p. 348.
29. Barth, *The Epistle to the Romans, op. cit.*, p. 50.

II. "THE WHOLE TROUBLE": ORIGINAL SIN

1. Karl Barth, "No!" in *Natural Theology*, with Emil Brunner, tr. Peter Fraenkel (London: The Centenary Press, 1946), pp. 116-117.
2. *What Luther Says: An Anthology*, ed. Ewald M. Plass, Vol. II (St. Louis: Concordia Publishing House, 1959), p. 3110.
3. David Hume, *Treatise on Human Nature* (London: Oxford University Press, 1911), p. 187.
4. T. S. Eliot, *The Family Reunion* (London: Faber and Faber Limited, 1939), p. 110.
5. "Good Grief, Charlie Schulz!" *op. cit.*, p. 27.
6. Salinger, *op. cit.*, p. 164.
7. Quoted in Williston Walker, *A History of the Christian Church*, rev. ed. (New York: Charles Scribner's Sons, 1959), p. 168.
8. Franz Kafka, *The Great Wall of China* (New York: Schocken Books Inc., 1946), p. 298.
9. Philip Melanchthon, quoted in C. L. Manschreck, *Melanchthon: The Quiet Reformer* (New York: Abingdon Press, 1958), p. 156.
10. "Knowing You Are Not Alone," *op. cit.*, pp. 8-9.
11. John Henry Newman, quoted in *The Wisdom of Catholicism*, ed. A. C. Pegis (New York: Modern Library, 1949), p. 652.
12. Barth, *The Epistle to the Romans, op. cit.*, pp. 85-86.
13. *Pascal's Pensées*, tr. W. F. Trotter (New York: E. P. Dutton & Co., 1958), Fragment 445, p. 124.
14. *Ibid.*, Fragment 451, p. 127.
15. Quoted in John Dillenberger and Claude Welch, *Protestant Christianity* (New York: Charles Scribner's Sons, 1954), p. 56.
16. "Good Grief, Charlie Schulz!" *op. cit.*, p. 27.
17. *Ibid.*, p. 26.
18. William Golding, *Lord of the Flies* (New York: Capricorn Books, 1959) p. 189.
19. H. A. Grunwald, ed. *Salinger* (New York: Harper & Brothers, 1962) pp. xvi-xvii.
20. "Good Grief, Charlie Schulz!" *op. cit.*, p. 27.
21. Grunwald, *op. cit.*, p. xvii.
22. *Pascal's Pensées, op. cit.*, Fragment 561, p. 155.

III. THE WAGES OF SIN IS "AAAUGHH!"

1. Quoted in H. Richard Niebuhr, "The Nature and Existence of God," *Motive* (Dec., 1943).
2. "Knowing You Are Not Alone," *op. cit.*, p. 9.
3. Barth, *The Epistle to the Romans, op. cit.*, p. 45.
4. "Knowing You Are Not Alone," *op. cit.*, p. 9.
5. "Ex Libris," *The Christian Century*, Vol. LXXIX, No. 25 (June 20 1962), p. 782.

6. Quoted in W. H. Auden, *The Living Thoughts of Kierkegaard* (New York: David McKay Company, Inc., 1952), p. 33.
7. Kierkegaard, *The Journals, op. cit.,* p. 363.
8. Will Herberg, *Protestant, Catholic, Jew,* rev. ed. (Gloucester, Mass.: Peter Smith, Publisher, 1960), ch. 11.
9. "The Anatomy of *Angst,*" *Time,* Vol. LXXVII, No. 14 (March 31, 1961), pp. 44 ff.
10. Eliot, *The Complete Poems and Plays, op. cit.,* pp. 58-59.
11. "Good Grief, Charlie Schulz!" *op. cit.,* p. 27.
12. Anton T. Boisen, "The Period of Beginnings," *Journal of Pastoral Care,* Vol. 5, No. 1 (Spring, 1951), pp. 15-16.
13. Søren Kierkegaard, *The Sickness Unto Death,* tr. Walter Lowrie (Princeton: Princeton University Press, 1951), p. 13.
14. *Henry V,* IV, i.

IV. GOOD GRIEF!

1. "Knowing You Are Not Alone," *op. cit.,* p. 8.
2. Kierkegaard, *The Sickness Unto Death, op. cit.,* p. 14.
3. Søren Kierkegaard, *Thoughts on Crucial Situations in Human Life,* tr. David Svenson (Minneapolis: Augsburg Publishing House, 1941), p. 1.
4. Quoted in Barth, *The Epistle to the Romans,* p. 39.
5. Kierkegaard, *The Journals, op. cit.,* p. 72.
6. *Christian Ethics,* eds. Waldo Beach and H. Richard Niebuhr (New York: The Ronald Press Company, 1955), p. 18.
7. "Knowing You Are Not Alone," *op. cit.,* p. 9.

V. THE HOUND OF HEAVEN

1. Quoted in Barth, *The Epistle to the Romans, op. cit.,* p. 24.
2. *Richard II,* V, v.
3. Kierkegaard, *The Journals, op. cit.,* p. 522.
4. "Good Grief, Charlie Schulz!" *op. cit.,* p. 27.
5. *What Luther Says: An Anthology, op. cit.,* Vol. III, p. 4910.
6. *Macbeth,* I, vi.
7. Eliot, *The Complete Poems and Plays, op. cit.,* p. 39.
8. *Van Gogh: A Self-Portrait, op. cit.,* pp. 189, 192.
9. Havelock Ellis, *The Dance of Life* (New York: The Book League of America, 1923), pp. 34, 62.
10. "Knowing You Are Not Alone," *op. cit.,* p. 9.

VI. CONCLUDING UNSCIENTIFIC POSTSCRIPT

1. "Knowing You Are Not Alone," *op. cit.,* p. 9.
2. *Pascal's Pensées, op. cit.,* Fragment 690, p. 195.
3. Kierkegaard, *The Journals, op. cit.,* p. 44.
4. Karl Barth, *Church Dogmatics,* Vol. I, Part I (Edinburgh: T. & T. Clark, 1949), p. 475.
5. Graham Greene, *Brighton Rock* (New York: The Viking Press, 1956), p. 357.
6. Graham Greene, *The Heart of the Matter* (New York: The Viking Press, 1957), pp. 296-297.
7. "Knowing You Are Not Alone," *op. cit.,* p. 8.
8. "Good Grief, Charlie Schulz!" *op. cit.,* p. 26.
9. *As You Like It,* V, iv.
10. Kierkegaard, *The Sickness Unto Death, op. cit.,* p. 3.